(continued from front flap)

The insights, experiences, knowledge, and conclusions gained over the ten-year period when the summer program was in operation form the basis of this report.

Written under the triple authorship (John Clizbe, Milton Kornrich, and France Reid, who have been closely connected with the Institute from the beginning, the study starts with the staff's and students' arrival on campus for one of the summer sessions. Of particular interest is chapter 2, with its detailed account of an entire day. Here the reader is given an inside view of both the morning staff meeting, with its analyses of the boys' progress, and the afternoon group therapy session, in which the kids have a chance to "sound off."

The chapters that follow break down the elements of the program's design, analyze the program's effects, evaluate what was learned about underachievers and the dynamics of underachievement, and discuss remaining problems and unresolved issues.

A comprehensive appendix section with such items as a schedule of a typical week; a sample psychological report; sample questionnaires to staff, parents, and alumni; an annotated bibliography; and a commentary by Dr. Kornrich on the confusing nature of recent "learning-disability" literature concludes this valuable study.

Written in clear, jargon-free language at conveys the enthusiasm, commitment, d, yes, excitement that the experiment ierated in all those involved, *A Chance Change* is that rare specialized book t makes fascinating reading for pro- ional and layman alike.

A CHANCE FOR CHANGE

A Chance for Change

Confronting
Student Underachievement

John A. Clizbe, Ph.D.
Milton Kornrich, Ph.D.
Frances L. Reid, M.A.

An Exposition-University Book

Exposition Press
Hicksville, New York

Contents

Preface

The human individual lives usually far within his limits.
He possesses powers of various sorts which he habitually
fails to use.

—William James

This report is about an attempt to deal with underachievement. It is an attempt that would never have been undertaken
or carried out without the deep personal commitment of its two
originators. One was Dr. J. Watson Wilson, a founding partner in
Nordli, Wilson Associates, psychological consultants to manage-
ment. The other was Mr. Francis A. Harrington, Vice-President of
the Paul Revere Life Insurance Company.

Early in his career, Dr. Wilson became aware of the great
waste of human resources that results from individual under-
production. In response to his interest in this problem, he
became involved in student counseling and curriculum development during his periods of work and study at both Muskingum
College and Yale University. World War II drew him into the
business world as a consulting psychologist, where he saw that
underachievement is by no means confined to the campus. In
the controlled and judgmental environment of industry, he was
able to learn a great deal about this common human phenomenon
and, over the years, made innovative contributions to the study
of motivation, interpersonal dynamics in organizations, and
human effectiveness.

One of his close associates was Mr. Harrington. As a business
executive, he knew well the difficulty an organization has in
establishing an environment which will tap fully the competence

of its members. He was also much concerned with the tribulations of individuals who are unable to live up to their potential. For many years he worked with Dr. Wilson on these and other psychological problems which occur in businesses as well as other segments of society.

In November of 1963, the two joined forces in a project that would crown their years of cooperation on a mutual concern. It had been apparent to them that, for many people, underachievement was a way of life; the underachiever could move away from it only as he was taught how to achieve. Traditional institutions were not geared to provide this kind of reeducation. In a plan responding to this specific need, Dr. Wilson saw the fruition of his academic beginnings; perhaps he could contribute to the educational world some of what he had learned in the business setting. For Mr. Harrington, the plan was an opportunity to focus his interests in a "grand experiment" in search of solutions. Putting aside the obstacles of practicality and the restrictions of scientific rigor, they set to work to translate their idea into action.

Within weeks, Dr. Wilson had involved other psychologists and educators and Mr. Harrington had gathered funds. Early in 1964, the Student Achievement Institute was incorporated as a nonprofit organization. Its purposes were:

Through teaching and counseling to help underachieving students achieve higher levels of personal effectiveness.

To conduct a summer program for underachieving students at a site to be selected.

To do research in identifying the causes of underachieving and to develop diagnostic and developmental methods and tools in the area of underachieving.

To publish research in the area of underachieving.

To provide training for academic and psychological personnel in dealing with underachieving students and their problems.

The summer program, conducted yearly from 1964 to 1973, became the primary vehicle for meeting SAI's objectives, emphasizing the pragmatic observations of its founders. It has also proven to be a rich source of observations and insights relevant to the concerns of parents, educators, practitioners in the helping professions, and underachievers themselves.

This report attempts to share the SAI experience, with the expectation that it can at least in part be applied to a wide variety of other situations, including "at home." For those who participated in this experience—staff as well as students—the subjective aspects of the Institute were often the most impressive. Therefore, this report records not only the arrangements, activities, and methods applied over those ten years—it also tries to communicate the successes, failures, lessons, hypotheses, interpretations, and hints which evolved. It is intended to stimulate additional thinking, applications, and research.

We dedicate this book to Dr. J. Watson Wilson, who provided the stimulus and the ongoing momentum, and who unfortunately did not live to see the results of his creative planning formally reported;

to Mr. Francis A. Harrington, whose spark enabled Dr. Wilson's ideas to take concrete form, and who faithfully shared with him the ups and downs of SAI's intense existence;

to the late Dr. William S. Piper, formerly Headmaster of Worcester Academy, who helped SAI become a physical possibility and who for two summers served as Executive Director;

to the students and their parents, from whom we learned;

to the dedicated staff of educators and psychologists;

and to those who served on the Board of Directors over the years, supporting the idea and the action.

The true "authorship" of this report is multiple, thanks to the generous response of former students and their parents and staff members—whose comments are liberally quoted throughout.

John Clizbe, the primary author, editor, and coordinator, spent several years as psychologist and/or Executive Director of the Student Achievement Institute.

Milton Kornrich served as a psychologist on the staff of SAI for several years. Having previously edited a major work in the field of underachievement, Dr. Kornrich's role in this report involved extensive writing, including some personal "questions, answers, questions," and a provocative query in the Appendixes.

Frances Reid was connected with SAI from its inception, serving initially as an assistant to Dr. Wilson. She has more recently had responsibility both for editing a great variety of original data and transcripts and for writing certain sections of this report.

We are very appreciative of the work done by John G. Holmes. He spent an entire summer on the campus with SAI, observing and participating in its activities. Significant portions of the manuscript he produced have been incorporated into this report—notably chapters 1 and 2, which are reproduced almost verbatim.

The authors particularly want to thank the other members of the current Board of Directors whose interest and encouragement were instrumental in compelling SAI to share its experiences: Mr. Frank L. Harrington, Sr., Mr. William D. Ireland, Jr., Mr. Laurence H. Lougee, and Mr. David N. Pynchon.

We are deeply indebted to Nordli, Wilson Associates, both for agreeing to "loan" the time of Dr. Clizbe and Mrs. Reid, and for the constructive assistance of the firm's psychologists during the writing process.

Special thanks are due to Janet Lee for contributing much of her own time and typing and retyping and retyping. Going well beyond this chore alone, her comments and editing have significantly shaped this final report.

A CHANCE FOR CHANGE

Introduction

A Chance for Change—
Questions, Answers,
Questions

If one function of time is to lessen "enthusiasm," enthusiasm of the sort that clouds more objective appraisal, then I and time have failed, for after six years, my enthusiasm for SAI remains and intensifies. We had something! The measurement-oriented reader may already be squirming, for how nebulous a term is "something."

How clearly my first contact remains. Our director, the late Dr. J. W. Wilson, had asked that the staff of five psychologists and five teacher-counselors arrive one week in advance. Dutifully, I left New York and my family on a late June Sunday morning (1967) and drove, finally, through a depressed portion of Worcester, Massachusetts. Others had not chosen to arrive this Sunday and I wondered what it would be like spending an evening in a hot, empty dorm (if the dorm was open!). Luck was with me, for one of the academic people and his wife, a couple living on campus, took in this stranger for drinks and dinner. I have always remembered their kindness. "Big city folk" do not usually expect such hospitality. So, over drinks and a

1

fine meal, I had an opportunity to discuss underachieving kids and, indeed, what kind of a psychological-academic program could be offered them.

Many problems occurred to me (and I'm sure to others) well before we met our first student. What would be the content of our six week program; and wasn't it naïve, even grandiose, to think we could offer anything of worth in six weeks? Well, it turned out that six weeks was not merely six weeks. In terms of treatment time, individual therapy three times weekly, group therapy twice weekly, combined with educational tutoring and multiplied by "the SAI milieu," I compute, seriously, the equivalent of a two-year effort. Six weeks—*our* kind of six weeks— could provide a significant wedge for further post-SAI work.

How would a new staff get along, and would it make sound, appropriate decisions? We found that the collective resources of the staff *did* frequently lead to very solid decisions. For example, the decision to have students take academic courses, which I initially felt would be rubbing salt in the wound, was absolutely necessary, since it gave us live, here-and-now data. I can tell you that it was a first for me as a psychologist to casually walk down the hallway during "study time" and personally observe the agonies of so many students in avoiding the task at hand. Never will I forget the student who dutifully sat at his desk, looked down at an open text, and frankly admitted to me that he was simply staring at the page. I jokingly stated at a staff meeting, we'd become famous if we could publish "How to Get an Underachiever to Read His Guide to Improved Study Habits Book."

Just as I had initial strong doubts about underachievers taking summer session courses, I and others worried about the ingredient in our program involving competitive sports. There were four teams competing for points in football, baseball, swimming, track, soccer, etc. One year, about midway through SAI's history, the "points concept" was expanded to include room inspection, violation of school or SAI rules and regulations, and academic grades at SAI. Rub competition into noncompeters? Crazy, right? Yet, it caught on and, despite the doubts of some that we were being too traditional and unpsychological, the competition seemed to have positive, energizing effects.

Would the students come in highly resentful of being dragged into "one more summer session" when they could be elsewhere? Why not underachieve in San Francisco . . . why come to Worcester for a hot summer and do the same? To my surprise, some students came, in effect saying, "Hey, I've blown it and I don't have a heck of a lot of time or options left. It's time I got on the stick." Others, of course, felt very much "dragged" and skeptical at first, but to the best of my recollection, only one remained that way throughout the summer.

Would parents expect a miracle? That is, "Here is my Robert, change him." And if not changed, did we foster false hopes? a rip-off? We found that parents, in most cases, did not expect a miracle. They were never promised one.

How would everything get "coordinated"? That is, we were guests of a private secondary school with nothing in the "contract" guaranteeing that non-SAI staff would share and support our ideas concerning underachieving kids. It turned out that although certainly problems arose and "coordination" was a major task, somehow our efforts caught the imagination and enthusiasm of many nonstaff people—from the Board of Directors to the teachers to the cafeteria workers to the community. We were particularly blessed with the consistent encouragement and wise guidance of our Board.

Could we really learn, really add anything from the experience? When I was given the assignment in 1967 to write a paper for the Institute entitled "What Has Been Learned About Underachievement?", I felt very uncertain. The role of so-called expert was not giving me pleasure. Yet, upon rereading that particular paper today, I feel that we did learn. Much of what we learned confirmed already existing notions.

Predictably, these questions and "answers" were only the tip of the iceberg, for there were daily questions—sometimes of a practical nature, sometimes theoretical. They produced a mountain of material, and not always what we or the measurement-oriented reader would most want. From this material, we hope the reader will gain some idea of the actual program, the questions and answers that emerged, and some "hint" of why we all concluded that our perhaps unreplicable, vigorous challenge to underachieving adolescents had a positive effect upon staff, student, and family.

If we could only communicate the intensity, the self-examination, the yearly changes, the conflict and the cooperation, the doubts and the joys . . . the hope of it all. My personal observation: SAI did accomplish one worthy goal—it provided all who participated, student and staff alike, "A Chance for Change."

MILTON KORNRICH, PH.D.

1

Arrival

Almost all of the boys will be apprehensive and anxious during the first few days when they are getting acquainted with us and our expectations for them. They will probably manifest this anxiety in different ways, depending upon the characteristic methods of adjustment they have learned. The aggressive boys may be somewhat more aggressive; the shy, reserved boys will be perhaps more so than usual. It will be up to the staff to handle these first critical days wisely and with the consideration of the individual dynamics of the boy together with an appreciation of the overall objectives and philosophy of the Institute.
—SAI STAFF OPERATIONAL OBJECTIVES, 1964

At first sighting, the back door entrance to the Academy's urban campus (a portion rented by SAI) is formidable. Three Victorian buildings present a stolid brick rump. The fence is high, the skyline dominated by a smoke stack—relic of an ancient heating plant. A student reacted this way:

The first time, we drove up behind the kitchen and it looked like we were driving into a prison. The whole place was surrounded by walls. It didn't look inviting. It got me scared.

Once inside, the campus opens up and welcomes a visitor with far more warmth and verdure. Three young, brick dormito-

5

ries simply and respectfully face their elders across four acres of well-kept grass. A large gymnasium and a theater built in the 1930's dominate one corner of the quadrangle. Shade trees edge the drive circling the campus.

The three dormitories were to be SAI's own. Two would be fully occupied; the third would be a useful spillover for staff. Everyday after four o'clock, the gym and playing fields were to be exclusively the province of SAI.

On Saturday morning the students arrived with their parents. Those who came a long distance were earliest to arrive, having spent the previous night in nearby motels; one came from Illinois, one from eastern Ohio, one from Michigan. The boy and his family who drove from Canada were the first to appear.

The staff had already been on hand for two busy days. Each boy had been assigned to one of four teams. The team psychologist and academic counselor carefully studied their students' folders that contained school transcripts, test-score data, interview evaluations, and other pertinent material. The selection criteria included (a) high average to superior I.Q., (b) no serious organic or psychological disorder, and (c) academic performance substantially below capacity.

There were exceptions, but these were calculated risks. One boy, accepted with an I.Q. of 105, showed several "deep pockets of intelligence" as well as "definite abstract and creative thinking ability." He had managed to get a straight and consistent zero in algebra for one year, a feat of some proportions in the eyes of the admissions staff.

As the families checked in, they were immediately scheduled for their first interview with the staff. Each family had at least an hour with the two counselors, who used the time to observe family dynamics and increase parental understanding.

Larry's father gave the firm impression that he expected the Institute to achieve a great deal for Larry.*

---

*Larry's individual experience will be followed through much of this report. The name Larry is a pseudonym. All materials attributed to him or about him did in fact pertain to a single student, but certain kinds of information have been omitted for the sake of anonymity.

Lee's mother cried during her interview. His father had stayed home, convinced the whole business was a waste of time and money.

Alan's father was charming and dominating. He sounded as if he were selling Alan, as he would merchandise.

Rod's parents overplayed their mutual esteem; a pall of insincerity hung over the performance. Rod showed a tentative look.

Howard's father had brought every test his son had ever taken, and he spread them out on the desk with a flourish.

Pat's mother, a bright and attractive divorcée, told the counselors that Pat's sole reason for underachieving was his adolescence and her divorce.

Steve's mother talked rapidly, articulately. Steve avoided looking at her and seemed to take little interest in what she said.

Glenn's father pointed to his wife and said, "It's all her fault. She has a personality conflict with him."

Gus hadn't wanted to come and two hours after arrival on campus was still in the car arguing with his parents:

> I was mad. I had just had a day's notice I was coming here— even less than that. I just didn't want to come. They had told me a month before they were not going to send me. This held until the day before the Institute, when I got my report card and they decided over again that I was definitely going to come.

This year there were twenty-nine boys from ten states, nineteen from public schools, ten from private. The youngest was fourteen, the oldest eighteen. The latter, a freshman in college, came alone, having made all arrangements himself, including financial. A taut, wary boy, he looked as if he might flee through the nearest door if anyone regarded him too intensely.

Sixteen plus was the median age. The full range of the middle socio-economic class was represented.

Larry, age sixteen, had signed up for SAI back in April:

> When I arrived, I knew this was an Institute that was to help me, but still I was a little apprehensive because I was afraid they might change me into some kind of mechanical being and I wouldn't like it.

At 1:00 P.M., Martin bid good-bye to his tearful mother. In treble tones, he promised to foreswear tobacco for the next six weeks. Her car was hardly through the gate when he lit up with a veteran's élan. Later that evening, he was water-bombed from a dormitory second-floor window by Neil and Tom. It was a direct hit and he appeared proud of his magnetism.

Tom had been almost as reluctant a drag-in as Gus. He consummated a last-minute deal with his father: He would try it here for two weeks; then, if he couldn't take it anymore, he could come home. There was no question in his mind about staying longer than two weeks.

Sam was walking alone, shoulders hunched like a little old man, but his eyes were alert, searching:

> I was looking forward to coming. I came on my own choice. I was having trouble in school. It was suggested by my parents and the guidance counselors at school that we ought to try another course in the summer. We did a little research; SAI looked interesting. I didn't know too much about it, but decided to come anyway.

Alan kept to himself, quietly reading Sartre's *No Exit*, wondering about the symbolism of the lesbian and figuring that he could just jog through this next six weeks and play everything his own way—real cool.

Chad had a police record:

> I decided it was about time I got something done. Before I didn't care about school or what it did for me. So I came with an open mind, willing to try what was put in front of me.

Bert:

> I didn't like the Institute at first, but I felt if I had to go away for the summer I might as well make the best of it. I didn't dig much of it the first few days, a week maybe.

2

One Day

Tuesday of the third week began gradually between 7:20 and 7:45 as the boys straggled into the Academy's dining room wearing varying mantles of wakefulness. By the time each one slid his tray down the serving rails and acquired a stack of pancakes, cereal, fruit, and coffee, his eyes were sufficiently focused to exchange greetings with the "Monster of the Day" who checked him off the breakfast attendance roster. The MOD, originally dignified as Master of the Day, by then knew all the boys and had a bantering word with most. His next chore was to unbed three others who did not show for breakfast. His approach was direct, as there wasn't much time before class, and rooms were scheduled to be inspected (at least above the disaster-area category) before class began. The prime incentive toward bringing room order out of normal chaos was the threat of losing points for one's team. Peer pressure had considerable effect, as the team would not take lightly losing half of the previous day's hard-earned football points against its closest competition simply because of one sloppy room. The team point-score sheet was closely watched each day.

The boys were scheduled to be in class at the Academy's summer school from 8:00 to 9:00, followed by an hour of study hall under the supervision of summer school instructors. Most were making up credit for a subject previously failed. These two hours were the "real world" wherein they had to cope with academic standards and demands.

While the boys were in class, the staff assembled for its regular meeting at 8:15. All were present except the MOD who arrived at 8:30 looking a bit grim. That day's disaster areas included two belonging to *his* team. An agenda had been prepared by the director and the first subject was how to cope with the lack of follow-through on specific student assignments. How much pressure were they to put on students to turn in a paper on time? What standards were they looking for in these papers? It was estimated that 85 percent of the students could not write a cogent one-paragraph essay. "Well, then," asked Mr. Gordon, "what is the objective for composition? Is it the idea, the imagination and/or skill in expressing same, or is it basically the grammatical construction we are after?"

Consensus to Mr. Gordon was: Forget your red pencil; encourage ideas, commitment. Don't worry too much yet about spelling, poor construction, and so on.

Other staff members expressed their points of view:

Mr. Jacoby felt the central purpose of SAI involved a concept of adjustment—the psychological problem to be solved at an intellectual level. "Let's not nitpick," he admonished, "there's too much weight to get in motion. Two weeks have passed; time is short."

Dr. Olstead said, "The students have two graphic phrases, 'He turned me off,' 'He put me down.' Both are explicit rationales for withdrawal. The kids must take responsibility on their own rather than let others quickly, easily, turn them off, put them down. They must be coaxed, even pushed, into taking positions. If we are going to hound them, it must be with much more subtlety, finesse, and patience than they are used to at home or at school. If we even imply to a kid that he is a fool, a slob, or a failure, he may well say inwardly, 'Thank God I've had my own opinion backed up by an expert I respect.' "

Consensus: Whatever techniques you use, do not let the student withdraw. Build from existing situation, encourage, give gradual opportunities to work through increasingly difficult achievements.

Dr. Donahue cited another difficulty: "There's a big problem on following up. It's easy to lose them in the tight schedule we have. There are a lot of ways they can duck. They can manipulate our forgetfulness."

Mr. Gordon added, "Forcing an immediate commitment is bound to start some momentum."

Consensus: Begin critique essays immediately following the achievement course lecture. Tackle at least one question, one idea—next time, two, maybe three—the "hierarchal" approach in brief.

Dr. Olstead, in closing the discussion, stated, "The Institute started yesterday in effect. The students have for two weeks been sizing us up, and each other. Now, it's for real. A student never gets going because he wants to. He's doing it for you. So we better move our asses—it's now or never."

The discussion lasted forty-five minutes. The chairman had let it go beyond the apportioned half hour, and then the staffing of students was continued. This is the process of acquainting the entire staff with background material on every boy. Nearly half had been done thus far.

Larry's team psychologist took the floor. His report went as follows:

Testing done with Larry throughout his academic career shows I.Q. scores ranging from 125 to 149. His most recent nonverbal I.Q. score was 130, yet he has consistently failed math courses. His other grades are typically C's and D's—and have been for several years, with his teachers commenting as far back as the third grade that he was not achieving up to his potential. He describes "study habits and learning skills" as his weakness. Teachers have complimented him for trying hard but his school indicates that he does not really seem to invest himself in his school work. The psychologist who evaluated his application indicated that he "certainly is not one to utilize all his analytical abilities." He is an outwardly stable and seemingly well-adjusted young man, though his elementary teachers had noted several years before that he was anxious about doing well and seemed to lack confidence in himself. Contacts with parents suggest that they tend to unwittingly focus on struggling against weaknesses rather than capitalizing on strengths. He seems to have short-lived interests and can be rather indifferent to his surroundings. He is very uncomfortable with the intense, hard-driving manner of his father, and seems to have expectations for himself which are quite a bit lower than those his parents have for him. He tends, however, to blame himself and to feel very unhappy and angry toward himself. He exhibits the intense and often conflicting needs typical of an adolescent—on one hand, the need to be independent and self-sufficient and, on the other hand, a need for emotional support and positive relationships with others. Note, however, that he vigorously rejects any interest in the kinds of social rewards which his parents seem to value. His insights do not seem to have much depth, and he exhibits the typical underachiever's reservations about really looking at himself analytically—though, if asked, says he will try. He may have stronger social skills than is typical of the underachiever, and adults in his environment compliment him in this regard. He seems significantly less sure of himself than others seem to see him.

Consensus for staff approach: Do a lot of work in individual psychotherapy concerning his attitudes toward his parents and his highly successful older brother; tap his apparent athletic ability; stimulate a positive attitude toward achievement; help him to demonstrate his untapped but very strong potential leadership skills. He will respond positively to adults who are frank and who level with him, and he needs adult support.

Other students were discussed with comparable "backgrounding," such as the report on Harry:

Harry is very bright, I.Q. approximately 130, but doing his best to make himself inaccessible. Dr. Olstead says almost every day to Mr. Thomas, in front of Harry, "Would you please introduce me to Harry?" to impress on him, by gag ritual, how hard he is trying to remain unknown within the Institute. He has missed half the group therapy sessions. He perceives things well but is unwilling to talk. He contains much unexpressed anger, characterized more by what he doesn't do than by overt expression. He complains that he feels overprotected and is treated like an only child. He is a good example of an anti-achiever. His active resistance to what is expected of him (i.e. achievement) reflects clear rebellion against what he feels is forced or pushed upon him. So, with a superficial, "I'm just lazy," he masks, "I just won't."

Recommendation: Get him into the physical contact arena (e.g., football, rather than solitary weight-lifting). Confront him at every opportunity.

Next, Dr. Olstead presented his picture of Steve:

Steve's parents are divorced. He likes his father who's not there, but has a bad time with mother. She nags him constantly on little things. He is far more disturbed than meets the eye. Rorschach showed roasted bugs, hanging entrails, all kinds of dead things. His wise-guy manner is obviously a facade. His teammates have assessed him as one-half great guy, one-half wise-ass bastard. He has considerable ability but much self-doubt. At the beginning, he would do anything outrageous to focus attention on himself. In his relation with the staff he starts with, "I'll show you by getting me," which posture is also a weapon used against his mother. He hasn't really been given much at home, so he feels he has to take. He is disconnected. He considers it a big deal to call adults by their first names, and feels this is important to him. He badly needs consistent relationships with strong male figures. Achievement is rejected because it appears phony to him in terms of his family and what he has seen of society. Success means making mother happy—and he asks himself, "Why the hell should I?"

Lee was presented next:

Lee is quite a mixed-up boy, but he seems to be in there fighting. "What is wrong with Lee? He's talking to himself." Kids seem to be aware of the battle he is having and there are definite evidences of protectiveness within the team in athletic competition. Steve, who is never one to withhold criticism, noticeably withheld punishment when Lee loused up a couple of important volleyball points. Only his mother came with him on opening day. She cried during half of the interview—really for herself and about herself, not for Lee. She released considerable anger at her husband who puts Lee down constantly. His mother is equally critical and probably oppressive. Lee is very bright, perceptive, suspicious, cautious and, having been exposed to numerous home battles, appears crushed. He had a very difficult time getting himself to interview Mr. Jacoby for the student paper. Finally, under considerable goading, he turned in a very good job. In general, he is most suspicious of teachers, labels them "weirdos," oddballs, and withdraws into his negative existence. Actually he needs a prep-school environment or, at least, to get away from home. He has considerable knowledge of cameras and electronics. He will not express anger directly; he mimics his teachers rather than criticizing them. He has no apparent ability to communicate, except with himself.

Then there was Howard, senior-to-be, very uptight, with everything either black or white. A guy is a real guy or a fag; a gal, a lady or a slut. His father is driven and driving—a real ulcer type and obviously working on one for his son. Howard seemed actually to be achieving beyond what tests would predict. He had an average of 88.6 at a school with low-medium standards. His verbal I.Q. is 109. His father was pushing him toward an Ivy League college, where he would hardly last six weeks, even if he could get in. He was accepted into SAI with full recognition that he was not an *academic* underachiever but was underachieving in most other aspects of his life.

Mr. Thomas commented, "We are now working hard on opening up additional possibilities for college. Howard wants to be commanded. He needs to be more anti-authority."

Dr. Olstead added:

I told Howard, "Do me a favor, will you? Don't say please." He does well on general information but falls down on reasoning or abstract concepts. He knows how to study within a weekly report system but cannot face exams, where he feels exposed. He is a very good athlete but not particularly liked by his peers. They are uncomfortable with his tensions and overwhelming urge to win at all costs. Since he seems to be reflecting the question, "Do you adults really care about me?" staffers should try to talk to him at every opportunity and show real interest in him.

There was much more discussion among the staff about all five boys. Dr. Ernest had two of them in his Red Cross Senior Life Saving Course and had useful observations on both boys. There were pertinent comments about their behavior on the camping trip this past weekend.

As it approached ten o'clock, the students drifted by the meeting room on their way from study hall. The staff adjourned with agreement that there would be a special meeting that night at 7:30 to catch up on student evaluations.

The rest of the morning was taken up with eight boys going to individual psychotherapy: four at 10:00, four at 11:00. Eight others had individual academic counseling on the same scheduling. For those with no counseling appointments, a movie entitled, *No Good,* running time approximately forty minutes, was shown in the lounge of the administrative building under the aegis of two "interns" from a local graduate school program in education. The film was an excellent picture of a boy, Eddy, age eighteen, about to get into serious trouble. He had "borrowed" a motorcycle, and the police were on his trail. A concerned social worker, his girl, and others try to get through to him, but he is enveloped in a miasma of fear and fantasies, strikingly shown in distorted flashbacks. The film was taut, dramatic, and well acted and directed.

The ensuing discussion was lively. "Eddy wasn't stupid, just foolish, not wicked but sure mixed up. . . ." "Family too poor for him to have things he felt he must have. . . ." "He got in deep when he tried to put his fantasies into real life. . . ." "How can a guy get along on one suit of clothes, fa' crisake?"

A counselor asked a question: "Can this type of situation apply in a middle-class environment such as ours?" He received a unanimous affirmative, leading to the suggestion of acting it out. The boys played their parts with real sensitivity. It was obvious that Eddy's predicament had reached them, and they responded with a minimum of prodding.

At lunch, the student council and its staff coordinator, Mr. Rollins, met for their biweekly session. There were four student members, one from each team. They saw themselves in an advocacy role. When they represented a student consensus on an issue, they had to convince Mr. Rollins, so he, in turn, would sell the idea to the staff. That day's hot potato concerned the dormitories during evening study hall and after lights out. There had been too much noise, horseplay. The question before the house centered on who was to supply the police force—students or staff—and on what kinds of weapons, if any, would be brandished—e.g., loss of team points, loss of individual privileges.

While this discussion continued, the staff of the student newspaper met briefly in another room. They had previously agreed to rule by committee—no editor-in-chief, managing editor, and so on. A staff member had been invited to attend in an advisory capacity. He was introduced by the academic counselor with the suggestion that his expertise would be useful to the paper, along with the implication that he should be asked to supervise. After a few uncomfortable moments and a bit of irrelevant rhetoric, the issue was solidly confronted by Larry, who said with some heat, "I thought this was going to be our paper, not Mr. Gordon's." The air was at once cleared, and the question of staff censorship got a hearing, followed by a brief discussion of format and production problems. Discussion of responsibility evoked a consensus for some operating procedures. The students would provide their own board of censors.

At one o'clock the teams gathered for the group therapy sessions. Team Blue was to go over the peer-self questionnaires which had been given out during the last session. These listed eighteen questions derived from the perspectives used in the final psychological report (described in chapter 3). Answers were marked on a rating scale which offered six choices. (The even number of choices required a commitment as to upper or lower half, with no easy straddle of the middle.) Each boy was asked to rate each of his five teammates and then himself. The team psychologists and the academic counselor also rated each boy, so there was a total of eight ratings for each one. Team Blue reacted conservatively: No one indicated a 1—the extreme at the poor end—and there were very few 6's, the top grade.

PEER/SELF QUESTIONNAIRE

(1)   How well does he think of himself as a person?

1	2	3	4	5	6

no good slobnik   the greatest, great guy

(2)   How would you rate his emotional maturity?

1	2	3	4	5	6

babe in arms (juvenile)   thoroughly grown up,
                                   solidly mature

(3)   How would you rate his independence?

1	2	3	4	5	6

leans heavily on others   firmly on his own feet

(4)   How persistent does he appear?

1	2	3	4	5	6

cops out quickly   stays with it to the end

(5) How much genuine self-confidence does he have?

1	2	3	4	5	6

has none at all   supremely self-confident

(6)   How flexible are his attitudes and opinions?

1	2	3	4	5	6
___	___	___	___	___	___

stubborn as a mule   great give-and-take ability

(7)   How much of his real self does he reveal to his friends
      and teammates?

1	2	3	4	5	6
___	___	___	___	___	___

impossible to dig   easy to know well

(8)   How well does he take fair criticism?

1	2	3	4	5	6
___	___	___	___	___	___

rejects it completely   very constructively

(9)   How much insight do you think he has into
      (a) his own problems?

1	2	3	4	5	6
___	___	___	___	___	___

thoroughly deceives himself   very deep and honest

      (b) other's underachievement?

1	2	3	4	5	6
___	___	___	___	___	___

couldn't care less   deep understanding

(10) How would you score his performance in a group
      discussion as to sympathy and understanding?

1	2	3	4	5	6
___	___	___	___	___	___

totally shallow or indifferent   great perception and warmth

(11) How well does he relate with the following compared with his peers?

    (a) *adults* (in general)

1	2	3	4	5	6

    (b) *his family*

1	2	3	4	5	6

    (c) *girls*

1	2	3	4	5	6

    (d) *young children*

1	2	3	4	5	6

entirely withdrawn   excellent communication

(12) If you knew nothing about his school work, what kind of grades would you expect him to be making?

1	2	3	4	5	6

miserably failing   top honors student

(13) How would you rate his academic potential for subjects in which he took a real interest?

1	2	3	4	5	6

hopeless   very high

(14) How would you rate his ability to stay with a subject in discussion?

1	2	3	4	5	6

loses interest immediately   very long interest span

(15) Do you feel that you could suggest any career for him on the basis of what you've seen thus far? Specify.____

_____

(16) Do you like him as a person?

         1   2   3   4   5   6

____   ____   ____   ____   ____   ____

the worst!   the greatest!

(17) How do you score him in
        (a) *leadership ability*

         1   2   3   4   5   6

____   ____   ____   ____   ____   ____

lowest   tops
        (b) *potential leadership not yet shown*
         1   2   3   4   5   6

____   ____   ____   ____   ____   ____

forget it!   tremendous possibilities
        (c) *sportsmanship in athletics*
         1   2   3   4   5   6

____   ____   ____   ____   ____   ____

the worst!   the best!
        (d) *as a team man*
         1   2   3   4   5   6

____   ____   ____   ____   ____   ____

couldn't care less   cares most

(18) How much do you think he is going to get from SAI?

         1   2   3   4   5   6

____   ____   ____   ____   ____   ____

absolutely nothing   enormous benefit

Date _____

Name (of rater) _____

Name (of person being rated) _____

Each student was given back his own self-rating sheet, in addition to the tabulation of what his teammates thought of him. The atmosphere in the small room was heavy with tension and concentration. They were almost immobile except for shuffling from one page to another. No one said a word for possibly three minutes. Sam was the first to show feelings. His self-scores were generally higher than those his peers gave him. The psychologist gently asked if anyone cared to comment on the relationship between the peer and self-scores. There was some stirring but no ready response. Finally, Larry, who had been conclusively rated the leader, said he was surprised at how high he was rated in self-confidence. (He had scored himself 3, and the peer consensus was 5.) This is a category that is relatively comfortable to discuss and it got a good airing. Their attitude toward confidence related directly to aggressiveness. The examples his teammates gave Larry were from athletic contests, such as, the way he came back after a bad error in softball and his ability to pick up the soccer team in a tough spot the week before. A question arose about determination versus confidence, which finally elicited the statement that Larry didn't always reflect confidence in group discussions requiring expressions of himself.

Larry stated later in the summer:

> I realize I showed them I had these potentials and it somehow built confidence for me because I could see that I wasn't just very un-self-confident since so many of them seemed to think I had something. I don't think it was an automatic thing but a gradual thing that I felt the leadership of the team.

Martin, the "scapegoat" of the entire Institute pecking order, was on Blue Team. At the first few group sessions, he had flopped soggily on the floor. His only contribution to the proceedings had been to light matches and burn papers in an ashtray. On opening day, his penchant for attracting trouble was already apparent, when he was singled out for water-bombing. At the peer-self session Martin was sitting up in his chair and he was "with it" (at least as far as Martin could be), partly because of the subjectivity of the moment, but he was also reflecting the time spent last week by his teammates discussing the whys of scapegoatism and how it could be coped with. He was probably surprised (and some others certainly were) to find that he had rated above average in popularity and potential for academic achievement and leadership. His self-rating showed a more modest self-esteem. That afternoon he may still have been a long way from manhood but he was functioning as a person and a team member.

Martin commented at a later date:

> I got to know myself a little better, my problems and how to deal with them. I guess when I came out here I was a little bit childish and I started to be the scapegoat of SAI, but then after a while I started to cope with these problems and watch my attitude and not act like a child any more.

Tom was in deep submersion. He was into something new for him. His reflection and concentration substantiated an earlier remark by his psychologist: "This guy is really hurting inside." He was rated very high in likability, leadership potential, and team dedication, but he drew a generally low consensus on emotional maturity, where he had scored himself a 5. That bugged him. He wanted to know on what basis his emotional maturity was determined. It transpired that he had squirted toothpaste on several people and had flopped down and gone to sleep on someone's bed during study period. He defended himself stoutly on those two points, maintaining they were isolated incidents rather than any kind of behavioral pattern. There was general skepticism toward this defense plea but his obvious sensitivity to criticism led to a remark that there had been discussions about his physique and that he was no longer looked upon as fat and overweight but rather as strong and hefty. A counselor added the accolade that staff members had commented on his speed and agility in athletics. The resultant glow could have warmed the room in wintertime. But they weren't through with him yet. Tom was taken to task for his tendency to bully, and then the group switched to Martin, his favorite target. "When Tom yells at you, don't yell back at him. You're just asking for more trouble the way you respond to him." Tom and Martin both listened intently.

Alan said later:

> In one of the team meetings we had, we picked one person out of the whole team and he just sat there and listened while the others took their turn and described what the person was to him. That is one time that made me really realize what I was. I was open for anything, good or bad. They said a lot of good things about me, and I didn't think there were that many good things. I guess I thought when I first got here that I was a real freak.

The session suggested that a team fabric was slowly being woven, perhaps more slowly than in other teams, but there was a distinct impression that each team member was grappling directly with his own needs and problems and that the counselors had established a definite momentum.

As always, the afternoon athletic program began with "individual events," with teams accumulating points on the basis of the improvement each team member demonstrated. It was an important fifteen minutes or so during the day, for it brought the team together in individual and common purpose for specific measurable accomplishments. There was just as much satisfaction and team glory, if you will, in an individual improving his fifty-yard dash from an 8.2 to an 8.1 as there was in a breakthrough from 6.0 to 5.9. Larry, at 6.1, was the same as the week before, but the counselors standing to the side noticed something very significant. He was running next to Martin, apparently "pacing him" and staying just ahead of him. Martin recorded a 7.1—a .2 improvement and, hence, two points for the team. Martin got a cheer and looked confused, but important, and Larry seemed to have a quiet smile on his face as he joined in the praise for Martin.

That afternoon, there was a touch football game between the two teams that were already battling for first place in the overall standings. Teams Red and Gold were a fair match, man for man, but Red had SAI's best one-two combination in Chad and Joe. They were both fast, passed well, and they worked smoothly together. Gold's Howard was no doubt the strongest player on the field and had the size and speed to pull down "the bomb" when the passer could get it to him. The rules allowed blocking and there was plenty of contact. Gold drew first blood via a long pass from Steve, which Howard grabbed almost in full stride behind the deepest defender, and there was no catching him. For the next ten minutes, the Reds moved the ball quite consistently but couldn't seem to find the key to scoring. Just before the half ended, Joe of the Reds intercepted a pass and took off down the sideline. The game was tied.

During the five-minute rest period, Team Red huddled closely, listening quietly as Chad outlined some new tactics. The Golds were arguing with each other. Mr. Thomas pointed out to them that Gus had been free on almost every play, that he had "good hands" and, with Howard drawing two defenders deep, would seem a likely target for shorter passes. Steve agreed, but Howard appeared unconvinced.

The second half was all Red. They scored three times: twice on sustained marches during which they mixed their plays beautifully, and once on an interception by Chad who took the ball away from Howard!

After that score, Howard stalked off the field without a word or backward glance. Mr. Thomas instinctively started over to him. Dr. Olstead said, "Wait, let him battle this one out himself." The teams waited awkwardly. The two staff members watched silently on the sidelines. The teams looked forlornly and imploringly at them for guidance, but counsel was really playing it cool. At last, Howard turned back to the field, his face pale and tight. "Come on, let's get going," he said stiffly but with conviction. On the next kickoff, they almost went all the way and the game ended with a fired-up Gold knocking at the goal line. Later, Howard said:

> Every time somebody made an error or missed a ball, I would scream my heart out at him. I guess that made them play worse. So I wised up and started complimenting them when they did something good. . . . I have found that a real leader should try to help out the other guys on his team. Now when they make a mistake, I try to help them out. This has made me a happier ball player.

On an adjacent field, a soccer game was in progress between teams Blue and Green. It was obviously a very close match and, since it was a new sport to many of the boys, those with the more "natural" athletic ability tended to stand out. Suddenly, there was a loose ball with Blue's Martin and Green's big Alex in hot pursuit. Martin was clearly outweighed by twenty pounds, and they were on a collision course. Martin dove to make a clumsy pass to Larry who, in turn, sailed in for a goal. Larry's teammates rushed to congratulate him but he, in turn, congratulated the prostrate Martin on his courageous coup.

After supper, there was a scheduled speaker. The week before it had been a basketball coach who talked about the relationships between achievement in sports and achievement in academic work. He spoke from his own personal experience, and the boys listened. This night, the speaker was Pete Gould, an SAI alumnus of the class of '66.

Pete, at age seventeen, came to SAI with a "things-couldn't-be-worse, what-have-I-got-to-lose" attitude. He said he was coming with a "half-open mind." With an I.Q. of 127, Pete had little trouble getting through elementary school with an A-B average and "not much sweat." In junior high his average fell to B-C. As a sophomore, his marks were in the C-D range, and he repeated eleventh grade. At fifteen, Pete was picked up on a charge of drunken driving without a license. His home environment was extremely poor about this time. An early questionnaire of unfinished sentences began: "My family. . . . . . ."; Pete finished the sentence: ". . . doesn't interest me." He had been promised a Honda by his father if he'd just shape up, but by the spring of '66 Pete hadn't "shaped up."

An SAI psychological study described Pete as "a young man of superior intelligence." There seemed little doubt that he "could" if he "would," but between the two lay a maze of poor study skills, carelessness, and inattention to details. He was suspicious of the motives of others—particularly adults. He hated authority and had an inordinate need for independence and self-sufficiency. "I don't like to be told what to do or to be pushed around."

To Pete, teachers were authority figures who were not particularly fair to him. If he felt a teacher was fair (and he there-fore liked the teacher), he worked at the subject and got good grades. In his sophomore year he flunked chemistry; he hated his teacher. ("She shows favoritism to people and if you get on the wrong side of her, you're in trouble.") Pete's way of "showing her" was by not working and flunking the course. At SAI, Pete's academic counselor persuaded him to vent his dislike of a teacher by working hard and throwing a good grade back at him for revenge. He tried this in chemistry, where he finally got a good grade and, when asked how it felt, said, "Oh, it was beautiful!"

Pete's proudest achievement at SAI was winning the Best Athlete trophy. He was sparked by seeing the trophies on dis-play, saying to himself, "I never won a trophy in my life." He was so hungry for one of those symbols that in the course of a week and a half he became a driving, purposeful competitor and leader. In somewhat simplistic terms, it seemed that his own collected, intensive focus on that trophy pulled him together as a person and, especially, as a leader. He said later that the night before the award he could have easily jumped out the window in a forecast of the despair he would have felt if he didn't win. Among other things, he had had to learn to control a violent temper and the implication of black moods of withdrawal.

At the end of the summer, Pete was accepted at a reputable private school. After a year there, he had turned in a creditable enough performance to be accepted for college.

Three years after his SAI summer, Pete was back to talk to the students. Along with an animal vitality, he manifested a curious mix of evangelistic fervor and self-dramatization. It made an effective combination to hold his audience's attention. "If it hadn't been for SAI, I'd be in jail right now!" They believed him. He described how he had learned to control himself and to use his energy for specific, discernible goals. Although he didn't use the word "hopelessness," the boys recognized the burden he must have carried in June, 1966. They wanted to know more about his relationship with his parents, then and later.

"First I shaped up; then they did. They saw I had changed,

so they treated me like an adult. We got an entirely new thing now."

This was an area they wanted to hear more about. He described the two weeks in September, 1966, when his family left him in complete charge of the home front.

"Before we'd have torn the joint apart every night. I'm not saying there was never a beer can opened, but there was, I mean, real moderation, man, and nothing or no one ever got broken up."

Later that night, dormitory bull sessions seemed to focus on growth instead of problems. More than one boy wondered aloud whether he'd feel at the end of the summer what Pete seemed to feel.

Was it coming together?

3

Confronting Student Underachievement

THE WHOLE

Underachievement is frustrating. Everyone is frustrated to see a child or colleague not live up to his or her potential. Not surprisingly, psychological research confirms the widespread suspicion that to underachieve is also frustrating for the underachiever.

Common observations such as these suggest that the Student Achievement Institute came into being in response to a timeless human problem. But its actual formation was stimulated by the rapidly changing, complex climate of the years since World War II. The tremendous expansion of knowledge, communication, and technology in general created mounting pressure for better education and, in turn, for better understanding and utilization of the learning process. It was gradually realized how much and how early a child learns *by himself* (in an organized milieu manipulated for his comfort and security) by observing, by feeling, by imitating, by experimental trial and error. It was also seen that many of the traditional methods and measures of learning are ineffective in helping this natural process and sometimes even hinder ultimate achievement.

Many attempts have been made to help students who run into difficulties as they struggle through the educational system. The scars left by a succession of failures are often very deep, however, and psychologists found that ordinary counseling and therapy were inadequate (or painfully slow) in getting a student started on a more satisfying path, even when he had no neurological impairment or severe emotional disturbance.

It was the total milieu which made the SAI summer program a profound experience for each student. All its techniques and methods overlapped to create this milieu. All overlapped as well in an effort to stimulate two critical ongoing processes for each student throughout the summer: first, self-examination and self-awareness and, second, self-stretching and experimentation.

The elements of the atmosphere were spelled out in the 1969 Staff Orientation Manual:

> Undoubtedly, the first, and perhaps the most critical, method of dealing with the students will be one of establishing and communicating the Institute's intent and environment. Based on our specialized objectives and theoretical foundations, such an environment would seem to include:
> 1. the fact that this is a unique and exciting experience;
> 2. the fact that this is a full time achievement-oriented experience where achievement is recognized, encouraged, and rewarded;
> 3. the fact that the experience is intended to be one of experimentation;
> 4. the fact that the students will be identifying with the Institute as a whole rather than with any special segment of the Institute;
> 5. the fact that the experience will be a demanding one which reflects our high expectations for the students;
> 6. the fact that, at the same time, we all feel assured that the student will succeed and we essentially guarantee that we will not "give up" on a participant;
> 7. the fact that the Institute is definitely helpful. We have the distinct advantage of virtually complete control over the environment of each boy for six weeks. We intend to use that advantage.

A number of basic concepts and assumptions, drawn from the areas of psychology, education, and everyday life, were utilized in translating the idea of SAI into a concrete program.

UNDERLYING CONCEPTS

A focus on the positive is more likely ultimately to "get somewhere" than a focus on the negative. For the underachiever, who habitually focuses on failure, it would seem appropriate to redirect his attention toward the antithesis of underachievement— that is, achievement.

Underachievement is a uniquely personal and frequently all-encompassing kind of experience. An individual's total self-concept builds and develops as he or she accumulates new experiences, new failures, new successes, new "amendments." A defeat or failure, particularly if built upon other defeats or failures, takes on meaning for the person, not just in isolation but in the total picture that person has of himself or herself. To confront underachievement, then, requires an involvement of the total person, not just an effort directed toward isolated segments of his life.

Furthermore, the causes and effects of failure and success are as uniquely individual as the person involved. The reason for one person's failure can be the reason for another person's success. One person aggressively seeks to prove that "I can *too* do it," while another person retreats in the face of the same challenge. One person compensates for a loss of hearing by becoming an exquisite artist, another becomes "permanently and totally" disabled. One person copes with the expectation of failure by setting impossibly high goals—"I'm getting an F so I'll aim for an A." Another person with the same kinds of expectations sets extremely low goals—"I won't get hurt if I don't try." One person angrily lashes out at and blames the boss or teacher or parent. Another person passively leans on the boss or teacher or parent for all the answers.

Given the breadth, depth, and diversity of the causes and effects of underachievement, it follows that any effort to "attack"

underachievement must have comparable breadth, depth, and
diversity. Underachievement is not a part-time experience; an
attempt to deal with it can be nothing less than an intensive full-
time experience emphasizing achievement and stimulating experimentation in the individual and those working with him.

Operating from the assumption that the underachiever has
probably learned to underachieve, it is necessary to provide an
accumulation of experiences which are incompatible with previously learned behaviors and fears. To accomplish this, it is not
only necessary to enlist the active involvement of the individual;
it is also necessary to provide an environment where achievement
is recognized, encouraged, and rewarded—an environment which
is a "model" for achievement. In such an atmosphere, the individual's efforts to learn and experiment and acquire new skills
can be reinforced.

The Student Achievement Institute's summer program evolved
directly from these basic assumptions and concepts. It attempted
to be positive in its orientation, total in its involvement, and
individualized in its approach. It sought to stimulate self-analysis
and self-understanding, and to create an environment which
enabled the student gradually to develop a new concept of
himself and to build on the experience of achievement and
success in a way which would generalize to new experiences and
concrete behavior changes.

A wide variety of psychological theories and techniques are
potentially applicable to this relearning process. Such eclecticism
can incorporate rewards and reinforcements encouraged by
behaviorism, the importance of self-understanding and self-dis-
covery emphasized by psychodynamic and nondirective psychological approaches, the interpersonal sensitivity encouraged by
communication theory and interaction-oriented theories, stress
upon reason and thinking of rational-emotive and other cognitive
psychotherapies, and a wealth of other orientations directed
toward the development of the individual.

The original summer program was designed in detail by the
founders. Each year provided new insights which influenced the
way in which the basic concepts were expressed and implemented.

Ten years of experience also reinforced and defined certain key elements of the day-to-day program which particularly helped to create the milieu and the opportunities.

CRITICAL PARTS OF THE WHOLE

The Psychological Evaluation

As many data as possible were gathered concerning each student as part of the selection procedure. He completed a series of multiple-choice personality inventories, an open-ended projective biographical instrument, a series of essay questions, and often other open-ended questionnaires. In addition, school records were obtained, including the results of tests taken by the student in his school settings throughout his academic career. Finally, a full psychological evaluation including an intensive interview was conducted, either by an SAI staff psychologist or another professional closer to the student's home.

With these data as a backdrop, the psychologist assigned to the student expanded the psychological evaluation through additional interviewing and testing after he arrived on campus.

The data were then organized into a format which psychologists on the staff had previously found to be particularly helpful in their work in businesses and schools. Students were "looked at" from six perspectives:

1. *Intellectual Characteristics.* What was the student's basic *degree* of intellectual capacity (not necessarily an I.Q. score but, rather, an overall capacity to think logically and comprehensively as assessed from a variety of perspectives)? What was the nature of his various *kinds* of intellectual abilities (for example, his relative skill with nonverbal versus verbal materials)? How did he *use* the abilities he had? Was he, for example, pragmatic or intuitive or analytical or thorough or imprecise, etc.?

2. *Emotional Characteristics.* How did he feel about himself and life-in-general? What particular kinds of feelings did he exhibit (for example, irritability or depression) and what were some of the dynamic factors contributing to these feelings? How

did he cope with his feelings? What was his typical mode of adjusting to problem-situations? How did he handle stress? and so on.

3. *Motivational Characteristics.* What was his basic level of energy and self-motivation? What degree of drive, personal ambition, and need to achieve did he possess? What were his important basic underlying psychological needs (for example, a need for affection or a need for self-sufficiency or a need for security)? On the other hand, what kinds of psychological needs did he strongly minimize or reject?

4. *Insight Characteristics.* How well did he know himself? How effective was he in reading other people? How sensitive was he to psychological kinds of variables in various situations? To what degree was he more self-critical than self-analytical or to what degree did he typically blame, rationalize, or project his feelings upon others?

5. *Skills in Human Relationships.* How did he interact with others? In what kinds of situations was he particularly skillful or unskillful? What kinds of followership or leadership skills did he have?

6. *Aptitudes, Interests, and Academic Skills.* What kinds of special aptitudes did he have (for example, mechanical aptitudes, special creative or artistic skills)? At this point in his life, what were his special interests? What kinds of study skills did he possess and how did he cope with academic situations?

These six perspectives were clearly to be viewed as six different ways of looking at the same individual rather than as unrelated "slices" of a person's personality. It was the task of the staff to develop as complete a picture of each student as possible.

Shortly after the opening of the summer program, the team psychologist went over each boy's evaluation with him, interpreting and clarifying it as the boy reacted to the reading. One boy stated:

I think the thing that impressed me the most was that you were able to sit down with your psychologist or your academic counselor and really talk to them and not hide anything, knowing that no one else would find out, because I feel very at ease when I sit down and talk to Dr. Andrews. I was never really able to sit down and talk to anybody and really tell them my true feelings.

From then on, the evaluation served as the basis for constant communication between staff members and between staff and student, as all of them directed their efforts toward more complete understanding of this person. The Staff Manual put it this way:

The crux of the Institute's psychological evaluation procedure is constant and continuing assessment and communication. Though conducted under the guidance of the team psychologist, all staff members are involved in the process of psychological evaluation all the time. Not an end in itself, assessment serves as the basis of *doing something* to assist a specific individual. Thus, the evaluation procedure must include the communication of observations and the utilization of this knowledge.

With the psychological study as the guide and stimulus, the staff planned a program specifically for each student.

At the end of the summer, a formal report was written which included the original descriptive evaluation, a progress report, and recommendations for the future. Since this was intended for the parents, both student and staff were extremely anxious for it to communicate well. On this depended the continuation or frustration of the boy's new growth. He and the psychologist worked together to put it in the final form. (See Larry's psychological study in Appendix C.)

We go over the report in considerable detail and, before the final section, "Summary and Recommendations," is finished, we ask each boy to make his own personal suggestions to his parents and we put them right in the report. Often they are most penetrating and projective of what we have been trying to get across.

All parents were expected to return at the conclusion of the summer program for feedback from the staff. This occurred in varying forms during SAI's ten-year existence. Minimally, a two-hour session was held, with the student present during part of it. It became increasingly clear that this amount of time was inadequate so, in later years, the contact with parents was typically much more extensive. In the final year, they were asked to come back to the Institute a day before it closed. A variety of experiences was provided for them: a meeting with their son's psychologist and academic counselor to read and talk over the boy's psychological report; staff-conducted sessions with groups of parents so that they could share feelings and experiences with each other; large-group sessions with a number of students and their parents present; and opportunities for parents to meet informally with each other as well as to talk with their sons. Finally, staff members met with each family in an attempt to initiate the transition "back home."

The last week was a tense and intense time for everyone at the Institute. Besides the usual schedule, it included preparation of the psychological report, final course exams, and the award banquet. Everything was permeated with the anxiety of anticipation—anticipation of learning the results of the personal risk-taking, the self-exposure, the sustained individual efforts of students and staff—anticipation of the end of a high-voltage experience—anticipation of the parental confrontation and return to the old life. There were big question marks hanging over everything. As a psychologist put it:

> Let's face it. The counselor and I are anxious ourselves. We have to convince the parents that there is still a long way to go for each boy and that most of the burden of responsibility is going to fall heavily on them. We have to convince them that we know what we're talking about. They must understand what we mean *in depth* and resolve to tackle what has been recommended. Some of the things we bring out are not entirely palatable, you know.

Yet, as another psychologist reported:

> Amazing, though, how well they can take the direct statement, "Mr. Brown, you must change your ways of dealing with your son."

Larry commented:

> In the choosing of values, society shouldn't push it on you. They should present their values, put them on display in front of you, and let you choose the ones that you want, by trial and error. You can take it and if you don't like it you can reject it, and you should also have your own set of values which you can make up on your own and not let society even present it to you. If you have something that society has not even heard of, but it is what you want, then it should be in your set of values.
>
> You have to examine yourself and you have to find out about yourself, know in what direction you want to go, and pick these sets of values by yourself. In the Institute here, I have gained insights into myself and I have a general idea of what set of values suits me best.
>
> The evaluation that the counselors have written is somewhat of a guideline, but I am still in the process of discovering things about myself and the types of values. I guess I will have to sort of wait for a conflict to come up and then try to settle the difference.

The Team

During the first four years, the team concept gradually became the primary instrument for translating SAI objectives into action. Almost all activities were built around the student's participation on a team, which consisted of about eight boys, a psychologist, and an academic counselor, and which competed against the other teams in a cumulative, summer-long, multi-event tournament. This constant association with a small number of individuals exposed the student to many strong influences, particularly in peer relationships, that could initiate and reinforce development toward constructive achievement. It called for direct participation in joint efforts with easily recognizable objectives. In these efforts, the more able could help the less able and thereby receive an immediate sense of achievement. The less able would receive encouragement as the strong supported them in their efforts to help the team. The reluctant would be stimulated by team spirit to try. And the close association of team members in group therapy sessions could lead to deep and meaningful insights. Larry commented:

> First of all, the business of relating myself with kids my age, and the sports activities, helped a lot. It was the team competition—doing the best for your team—that sort of brought out the best in each individual. If we didn't have the competition, a lot of energy maybe would have been wasted, wouldn't have been brought out. Also, being involved in group therapy sessions did a lot in understanding guys better and it wasn't just a superficial meeting with kids, like you have in a regular school system—I mean, when you're just there nine to twelve and one to three, that's it. Here, you are with them twenty-four hours, and this is sort of a new experience and I really enjoyed being with the kids twenty-four hours.

For the staff, too, the twenty-four-hour-a-day involvement in the problems and progress of their team would provide innumerable and inescapable occasions for evaluation of their own skills and development. One staff member reported:

> On a personal level, I found the SAI experience extremely helpful, both in terms of bringing me to a fuller awareness of myself and also helping me develop some ideas I've been able to transfer to my regular work.

Utilizing all of the psychological and academic data available for each student, one of the major pre-Institute staff tasks was dividing the student body into teams. Several criteria were applied: intellectual balance and diversity, physical and athletic balance, special skills of staff members, staff members' "comfort" with a particular kind of student, the probability of one particular boy benefiting from contact with another particular boy, and so on. There was certainly a degree of guesswork.

Each year, the early weeks of the summer session were crucial as the staff tried to start the growing-together of the team. From a heterogeneous collection of bright, suspicious, defensive boys, there had to evolve a mutually supportive unit—a "family," so to speak, whose success depended on the individuals and which, in turn, promoted their well-being—whose members communicated clearly to each other and thereby encouraged understanding of self and others and elicited a spirit of cooperation and loyalty.

The teams operated under a detailed point system. A team received ten points for team victories in five sports; one point per unit of individual improvement in speed, strength, and agility tests; every two weeks, for improvement in composite academic grades, the highest team earned fifty points, the second, thirty, and the third, ten. Points were also awarded for special individual improvements. In addition, a room that failed in the daily inspection cost the team five points. Other means of building team points were announced from time to time. The relative standing and point totals of the teams were posted daily, and it was made clear from the start that members of the winning team would receive awards at the end of the summer.

In the early years, the athletic program was primarily recreational, but it developed into an important medium for implementing the team concept. Team sports were touch football, volleyball, soccer, basketball, swimming, and track meets. Each team played every other in a tightly scheduled round robin and, with only eight to a team, every boy played and every game counted. The setup developed team incentive and, of equal importance, individual self-competition. Prior to the scheduled team sports each afternoon, there was a warm-up calisthenics session on the grass for ten minutes, followed by individual track efforts. Then, at least twice a week, each individual was tested for the team's record in each of the following events: 50-yard dash, with one point for one-tenth of a second improvement in individual time; 100-yard relay run, with one point for one-tenth of a second improvement in team time; standing broad jump, with one point for every inch improvement; pull-ups from the limb of a tree, with one point for each additional chin-up; and several other specially designed events.

Every year, there were boys who were reluctant to take part in the athletic program. There was no way for them to avoid it, however, and in most cases, as they found they weren't the only ones who weren't very well-coordinated or didn't know how to play soccer, and as the team feeling began to take hold, they began to enjoy it. As team spirit intensified through the summer, the whole team was likely to be on hand during the "For the Record" tests of individual athletic accomplishment. As one of the boys commented:

> The athletic program wasn't really too bad. Some days I really didn't feel like playing, but I had to anyway. Once you get into it, it is sort of fun, the team spirit gets to you. The team concept is a good idea because everyone works together and you get to know some of the kids better.

All this group effort led, in the end, to the banquet when the winning team received an award.

Academic Work

In most cases, poor academic performance was the immediate impetus that brought students to the Institute. They all needed to earn credits or make up failures for their year-round academic program.

Throughout SAI's history, each boy took at least one academic course in the summer session of the school on whose campus the program was held. He received no special attention during class time and had full responsibility for his grade. Usually the subject was dictated by the requirements of his regular school, but often a boy was encouraged to take an additional course without credit—one that would give him a chance to branch out, to satisfy some curiosity. In addition, every student took a special course, taught by the SAI staff, in Psychology of Achievement in Life. This ran throughout the summer, helping to provide an intellectual understanding of the experiences the boys were having. It also provided a situation over which the staff had control for the improvement of academic techniques and skills.

The student's sessions with his academic counselor were

aimed at remedying the student's particular weaknesses in study skills. The academic counselor also helped him set specific objectives in his daily activities—objectives that were not so high that he was setting himself up for failure and not so low that he was copping out. He might aim at a D+ instead of a D in his next French dictation, or he might get his outside reading done a day ahead of time instead of arriving at English class with it half done. It was in the academic sphere that particular emphasis was placed on setting achievable short-term goals and on taking manageable "small doses." Frequently, especially at first, students were told to study only—and no more than—fifteen minutes, but to use that fifteen minutes well. Most students rarely got in more than fifteen minutes of real study anyway; when sent to their room to study for two hours they worried the first hour about what to do and the last hour about what hadn't been done. Gradually this fifteen minutes could be increased.

Each boy kept a running record of his day-by-day objectives and his progress toward them, of his insights into ways for reaching short- and long-term goals.

But in the academic area, even with team pressure, it was very difficult to initiate study momentum. Here, the boys in SAI had long since established strong antagonistic reactions. As a staff member said:

> We've heard from just about every academic counselor—and it certainly was true in past years—that there is a strong resistance to head-on academic work sessions. You guys report you have to walk around this problem and come in from another door to establish even a level of discussion. It's not just that it presents a threat; it's more that it triggers a well-trained reaction to a dismal, miserable, traumatic set of experiences. So what do we do?

Here came into play one of the basic considerations of SAI: Almost all students were underachievers in every aspect of their lives—academically, athletically, socially, and so on. If underachievement is seen as a generalized behavior pattern that involves the whole personality of the individual, then improvement in academic performance might well be expected to appear simply as one result of a deep-seated change in attitude. When a person develops understanding of himself, his feelings, his abilities, and his habitual ways of using them, when he experiences the feeling of achievement and realizes that he can achieve in some area— any area—then it is possible for him to go on to success in other areas. Larry reported:

> I just told them I was tired of losing all the time, that I wanted to win. I think the past few weeks we really worked together as a team. We started to win a lot of games. That made me hit the books harder, too, because I felt more at ease and a lot better, too. People were telling me that I did real well in sports so I thought I could not only do a good job in sports but also decided to do a good job on the books.

In the simultaneously challenging and supportive atmosphere of SAI, the *feel* of achievement was communicated. As the boy experienced it in any area, no matter how small, his success was rewarded, reinforced, built upon, to develop his appetite for it. The summer school course was an opportunity to get that "feel" of success in the academic area. It was, of course, a tentative one—a trial while the necessary attitudes and skills were only beginning to be accepted—while there were many habits and conflicts holding him back. It was not the kind of achievement that could follow instantaneously upon a breakthrough in the fifth week. Grades had to be built up by effort through the whole summer. It was hard to get it going early enough. Martin commented:

> I don't think in academics I really benefitted. I don't think I have had enough time to sit down and think about it. I have had a lot of problems with being a scapegoat, dealing with my problems, and that has taken up most of my time. I got the scapegoat off my back for nearly two weeks now, and now I just sat down with my work and I am working on my final. . . . I think now I will sit down and get organized, but I still think I will need a little more help. I think to get settled I need a little more of a person standing on my back and making sure that I do my work. I guess I will get into the hang of it. They

won't have to hound me any more. . . . I think my counselors have been a little rough on me so that I can get down to work. They have accomplished letting myself know me.

So it was not surprising that truly good academic grades were uncommon. Even so, the point system monitored improvement every two weeks, and the end-of-summer awards recognized notable change. In looking back upon the program, another student said:

I felt the psychologists were going to give me a lot of garbage that I have been given before, but I gave them a try and they really helped me. . . . Mr. G. was kind of strict, but I guess that helped me know I had to get the work done.

Psychotherapy

Most students had had some sporadic psychotherapy, tutoring, or remedial reading help before they came to the Institute. But although most came from financially comfortable families, very few had received any *consistent* professional assistance.

Individual and group therapy sessions were always a vital part of the SAI program. The amount of time devoted to this activity varied somewhat from one year's schedule to the next, and from one boy's needs to those of another.

In the group sessions, the team was exposed to an amalgamation of group therapy, sensitivity training, and committee-conference techniques. Early in the summer, if things went well, the boys began to recognize each other's needs and hang-ups, strong points and sensitive spots. They began to hear comments as useful data instead of threats, and to open up about their own feelings. It took all the insight and skill of the team's psychologist to start these less defensive attitudes working. The other experiences of the team under the direction of the team's counselor fed into the process. From a staff member:

_____, as my team co-captain and now friend and colleague, helped me immensely in my struggle to "achieve" as a therapist with our seven kids. He provided a willing, involved, and steady consultant to me as well as an active, sensitive team partner. I'll always be grateful for this experience together.

The individual therapy sessions with the psychologist, beginning with discussion of the evaluation, helped the boy to confront himself, to understand his own true capabilities and what he had been doing with them. From a student:

> I think that really when I came here I thought I was terrible and everything, and the first thing that Dr. A asked me, I think, was what do I think of myself. So, I don't know how he did it, but—you know—I didn't understand how it was going to help me get along with anyone or get along with myself. I just didn't understand what was going on. And I asked him how this was going to help me and he just didn't say anything. He kept right on going. I think about three weeks ago I started to realize that I never really hated myself that much; I was just hating what I was doing in school, with my parents, and everything else. I really think a lot more of myself now and I value myself a lot more than I did when I first came here. I would suggest for anyone that came here in the future, they would have to be ready to cooperate with whatever is going to happen and they would have to remember to just keep thinking about themselves that they are not as bad as they think they are. I think that is what I did and I think that if anyone else did that they will end up okay.

Time limitations directed the individual therapy sessions toward a behavior-change orientation combined with development of self-awareness, rather than digging into problems which could not be worked through by the end of the Institute. Behavior change was, of course, the object of the basic concept of providing many small opportunities for achievement and then rewarding their accomplishment. Another fruitful approach was to develop behavior patterns which were incompatible with the student's habitual ones. He could learn, for example, to respond to situations actively instead of avoiding them, or to be relaxed instead of anxious. The aim was to establish adaptive responses which would automatically prohibit old self-defeating ones.

But it became quite clear in the early years that "psychotherapy" could be defined and applied in much less traditional ways, with the staff interacting with the student at times and places other than the formal sessions in the office. As one staff member said:

> I would like to appraise this summer's Institute from the stand-point of communication. By communication I mean the ability of the students to communicate with the staff and vice versa. Actually, there are three different paths for communication at the Institute: (a) student-student, (b) student-staff and vice versa, (c) staff-staff. The most significant of these, therapeutically, would appear to be the student-staff pathway and here I would say that the Institute was extremely successful. I think the students' overwhelming positive appraisal of the therapy sessions is evidence of this, as is the way they seemed (at least in our group) to be better able to communicate with their parents. I do not mean to imply that the individual therapy sessions are solely responsible for opening the lines of communication between these kids and adults; in fact, I believe that quite the contrary is the case. I feel that the lines of communication are really opened up on the sports field, the pool, on Mount Monadnock, in the car on the way back from Expo, etc., and the insights gained here only become clarified in the therapy hours.

The exchanges on these excursions, as well as many others back on campus, were examples of what one psychologist called "back porch therapy"—unplanned, informal, capitalizing on the situation of the moment. He said:

> I caught Bud on the way back from lunch today and, as you suggested, asked him why he always has to play the clown. You're right. He has no idea how bright he is. As we anticipated, his answer was, "Well, you do a lot of clowning around yourself." So we had a go at the Pagliacci bit. Think I got through to him on the difference between clowning to hide something and horsing around to stimulate others.

Two other therapeutic activities deserve mention. One was bibliotherapy: reading literature which could offer the boy insights into his particular problems. An extensive reading list (a portion of which is described in Appendix F) was made available. Sometimes a student took "pot luck," sometimes books especially relevant to his unique condition were prescribed.

The other, as a Staff Manual pointed out, was "achievement-oriented sleep!"

Specially Designed Extracurricular Activities

In addition to the basic activities of the SAI day—academic work, athletics, and therapy—there were, every year, what might be called extracurricular activities. These, too, were designed to provide impetus and opportunity for achievement. Some proved effective and were repeated in most of the ten years.

One of these was a Red Cross Senior Lifesaving course. It is perhaps best described in the words of the staff member who conducted it.

In the years we have had the Senior Lifesaving course, about a third of the Institute, roughly between ten and twelve boys, turn out and are successful in completing the course. It is strictly voluntary; in fact, the boys have to give up what would otherwise be free time to participate, and it is made clear to them at the beginning that they are going to have to give of themselves not only physically, but mentally, as well, in terms of reading and mastering a textbook and taking a demanding final examination.

To the boys, the appeal is threefold: (1) There is some prestige in taking senior lifesaving and getting the Red Cross patch; (2) it opens up job possibilities both in summer and winter; and (3) it gives them a sense of achieving something worthwhile within the six weeks here. We get closure on something that started when they came. In many cases, they are surprised at being able to complete it.

In terms of interpersonal relationships, we feel it emphasizes many of the areas we are trying to deal with in the Institute. One, of course, is confidence in one's ability to perform in situations of stress. Certainly the final water-work exam is a stress situation in that the instructor, as victim, places himself in different predicaments to which the student must respond instantly and appropriately. We also find the written exam useful as an academic tool. Designed by the instructor for the Institute, the exam includes many different types of questions: multiple choice, true and false, short answers, and essays, giving them some experience they may not get in regular academic work. . . . There can be opportunities for directly relating the water experiences to psychological counseling: faith in himself, sticking with it, the necessary focus on essential details rather than approaching things in a global or superficial manner.

An example is a student two years ago who in every other way was an extreme behavior problem at the Institute. He was at many times close to being expelled as a chronic absentee from classes, study hall, appointments, etc. He approached the lifesaving course with a great deal of vigor, and became genuinely involved in this one area despite himself. This was a youngster considered rebellious, flunking the program in every other way. The lifesaving gave his psychological counselor an opening, pointing out to him that once he did get involved he was able and equipped to do very well. This boy came on fast in the last two weeks and surprised a lot of people.

We have noticed that many students come to the Institute without any idea of how to care for another person. One of the first things we do is pair them off with one another according to size and compatibility. As the rescue techniques proceed, they learn a great deal about caring for the other person, considering how he may be feeling, what may be going on in his mind. We try to give them insight into the behavior of a victim— whether he be panicky, passive, cooperative.

Also, we have noted that many boys come here with concern about body contact, reflecting natural midadolescent anxieties over any kinds of sexual feelings aroused as a result of male contact. Many students feel uncomfortable with this contact in the beginning but, by the end of the course, it has all disappeared with an awareness of the context of the situation and no need to question their own masculinity. In sum, I believe that lifesaving offers a very good laboratory-learning situation where we can approach many of the personal and academic problems that boys face when they first come to SAI.

Another extracurricular activity which was included in the program annually was the camping trip in the mountains. The symbolic value of a physical climb to the summit of a mountain appeared in the very early planning of the SAI. Most years it took the form of a long weekend excursion, held early in the summer, and provided a natural testing ground when students and staff were still feeling each other out. Each expedition included two teams—small enough groups to reveal each camper both as an individual personality and as a part of a group.

An occasion such as a camping trip challenged the staff professionally as well as physically. It is true that the entire six weeks was strenuous for them—always pressing them to make the most of every contact with a student—straining their resourcefulness to make every conversation meaningful—but the trip's requirement of common effort and ingenuity led to moments of closeness that were special opportunities. Here again, the words of a staff member describe the experience.

I think that the experience was one of the most worthwhile things done at the Institute. To move into a setting such as we had at Franconia Notch with a reasonably small group of boys provides them with a "doing" experience that both brings out their individual personality characteristics and also gives observers a good insight into how well they do or do not work with each other. It also gives the adult team leaders a good chance to establish an intimate relationship with the boys as individuals, as well as with them as a group. The chance to swim, do some climbing, take off-time trips into town, sit around the campfire and chat, cook the meals (if some of those guys had to cook their own meals they would starve!), do all the things connected with trying to set up and make comfortable a few days of living together . . . all were excellent means of bringing the teams together as units. The long July Fourth weekend seemed an ideal time to do this.

There is nothing like sharing a creative experience to break down the barriers between boy and man. I found that putting up a tent, cooking meals, toiling along while trying to appear in the peak of condition climbing the mountain (I really love it), driving back and forth to town, trying to figure out how some of the boys were going to stay warm . . . all these things served to establish a natural means of relationship between the boys and group leaders. You very quickly find out in such a fundamental experience who are the doers and who are not. Everyone has a chance to prove himself, and some really surprise you. For example, Pat had shown himself to be somewhat standoffish, but on the camping trip he stepped right in and helped with everything and was especially good at cooking. Gus showed himself to be both persistent and patient in the little episode where he was trying to trap chipmunks under a cardboard carton he had propped up with a stick to which was tied a long length of string. Try as he might, the trap would fail to work right, but he always tried again. Howard revealed himself to be uncertain, excitable, and to really have a difficult time relating easily to his peers. He found it hard to volunteer his cooperation in the various chores around the campsite. Steve just continued his little boy antics, always clowning around and being a pest. Harry showed a lot of stubborn determination, in that I know it was difficult for him to climb over the four peaks of the Lafayette

Range; but he stuck with it quietly at his own pace and finished along with everyone else. Lee was just Lee. Particular comments on the other team escape me, except that I found the trip an occasion to get to know the other team's members far better than otherwise might have been the case during the summer. . . .

One type of extracurricular activity took a variety of forms in different years: working with underprivileged or handicapped individuals. One summer, some of the boys went regularly to a state mental hospital to visit with patients. Another summer, a group of young children were brought to the campus once a week from an orphanage. Each one was assigned to a certain SAI student for the whole summer, so a kind of "big brother" relationship developed. The preparative material for the boys might include something like the following:

> They have generally not known success in any area of their lives. . . . Any lessons will probably have to be less formal and more of the fun type. . . . Don't worry about not accomplishing a great deal here; just their contact with you will be beneficial. . . . Reading is the most important subject at this level. Start with what they can do and then encourage them on to higher performances. . . . Above all, be warm and receptive. . . . Respect their beliefs and don't try to disillusion them. . . . Change the pace often; their attention span is usually limited. . . . The atmosphere should approach that of a camp, not of a school. This is their vacation time.

These experiences meshed with the achievement-oriented design by stretching the student to help someone else, by showing him how someone else reacted to difficulties, by helping him experience the impact he could have on another life, and by giving him the experience of working with someone instead of being "worked with" himself. Three boys commented on this activity:

Larry:

> We were making kites and I figured out a new way to put a tail on. It really took off and they looked at me like I was some kind of genius.

Pat:

I'm more or less a loner. I like to stay by myself. These kids gave me a feeling of importance, that someone really wanted me and wanted me to do things for them.

Harry:

On the first day, my little kid came up and put his arms around me and talked and talked. Later, I found out he came from a broken home. Made it easier to understand.

Even though the staff was only marginally involved in the meetings between SAI students and their young protégés, they tried to learn from them. As the visits were about to begin, one staff member wondered: "If we carefully observe the methods the underachiever uses to tutor the child, could that 'clue us in' to possible tutoring approaches with the *underachiever?*" Although they failed to organize a formal research project, a number of staff felt that their observations provided many clues concerning the boys' feelings about younger siblings, females, being the "authority," and so on.

Individual projects were designed to capitalize upon an already existing interest. One boy. who for most of the summer was closed to all efforts to establish rapport and seemed interested in nothing but hard rock music played at maximum volume, was finally reached through that very medium. He was set the task of communicating the meaning he found in hard rock to the squarest of the staff members. He formulated the subject and evolved a mini-course in it, complete with explanations and examples. Proof of his success came when the staff man asked for a taped copy of one recording; he liked it and wanted to expose his wife to it.

The whole system was geared toward encouraging and rewarding individual self-development, helping a boy realize he had some control over his own destiny and could influence events through his own efforts. One of the students reported:

Before I left home, I told Doris that the only reason I was coming here was because of her, so that we could have a happy future together. I guess I said it because I didn't want to do anything for my parents after they were nagging me all the time about Doris. But I guess about the fourth week I realized that I was doing it for myself and for my own satisfaction, because I wasn't only living for Doris, I was living for myself.

It helped me realize everything is up to me. . . . I feel sports have helped me immeasurably. And I realize everything is up to the individual person.

Staff

One principle which was never questioned was the value of a highly competent staff. From the earliest plans to the last summer session, experienced psychologists with doctorates from first-rate universities directed and carried out the psychological aspects of the Institute. The academic counselors were experienced teachers with a particular interest in the problems of gifted students, recruited from the faculties of private and public secondary schools.

In the selection process, all of them underwent not only scrutiny of their records and references, but also the same kind of psychological evaluation as the students.

All this was in the interest of finding competent, stable, strongly motivated people who were both innovative and team-oriented, insightful and gregarious, physically active and intellectually solid! They needed to be men who could provide viable models for the groping students. For this reason if no other, it seemed highly desirable to have former underachievers on the staff.

The junior psychologists who were employed in the early days, as well as people who worked in various other roles from year to year, were also chosen carefully along more or less the same lines.

Staff effectiveness varied, of course, from one year to another. Some groups seemed to work particularly well together. On the other hand, there were a few individuals who turned out to be less well suited to the rigors of forty-two days and nights of intense association with some thirty struggling adolescent boys and perhaps eight opinionated colleagues.

But the importance of a superior staff cannot be overestimated —superior in their qualifications for translating the purposes of the Student Achievement Institute into action, superior in their ability to see and analyze and make use of the results of their actions. On the staff's ability and skill rested the chance for change for those thirty boys, and for many other people who would be touched by that summer experience.

Methodological Evolution

Many of the methods and techniques evolved through the ten years of SAI summer programs. They were far from static and, in fact, were never intended to be. They were discussed in staff meetings, commented on in the annual staff assessments of the summer just finished, altered experimentally, altered again, changed in emphasis, discarded.

The change in formulating the team concept was quite marked. Although the value of teams in transmitting peer influence was clearly recognized from the beginning, they began as purely intellectual groups, called "learning teams," each one charged with investigating some aspect of achievement or lack of it. During that early period, the composition of the teams changed every two weeks. By 1968, it was clear that keeping the teams as permanent units all summer for all the activities had a much greater impact. The closeness which developed among team members and the cooperative effort to bring glory to the team seemed much more likely to build up self-understanding and the desire to achieve.

Even the basic "milieu" concept changed somewhat. It was clearly present in the original planning in terms of round-the-clock immersion for the students. But at that point, the various activities were not thoroughly integrated to reinforce each other. Although all were aimed toward achievement, they tended to be compartmentalized: therapy versus academic work; learning team versus recreational athletics; senior psychologists living off campus versus psychological interns manning the dormitory.

After a few years, as the team became the unifying concept of the arrangements, with *everybody* involved in *everything*, the cumulative effect of one unbroken environment was brought much more completely into play. In the beginning, students could take two weekends away from the campus; in later years, they were required to stay with the groups straight through the six weeks.

The evolution of the integrated milieu was accompanied by great changes in staff roles. The compartmentalized nature of the original arrangements extended to the staff responsibilities. There were senior psychologists who handled the individual psychotherapy sessions, lived off campus, and were less involved in the myriad day-to-day activities than the junior psychologists. The latter were graduate students in psychology who ran the group psychotherapy sessions, lived in the dormitories, and were close to the boys' everyday lives. The academic counselors were basically teachers, concerned with traditional student areas: classroom, athletic field, dormitory.

These role distinctions diminished, however. It was soon realized that the psychologist's influence was tremendously increased if he and the boy were interacting all day long. This led, among other things, to the eventual elimination of junior psychologists. Every psychologist had to be professionally advanced enough to handle all aspects of the boy's psychological development. One staff member commented:

> In the past three years that I have been at SAI, there has developed strong tradition of the psychologist's role being multifaceted. Those psychologists, be they senior or junior, who have had the most difficulty at SAI have been those unwilling or unable to climb out of their traditional roles as psychologists in an office or hospital setting.

There was realization also that concerned academic people had a great deal to contribute outside of their teaching roles. He continued:

> I think that more teachers need to become aware of the vital non-subject contributions that they can make to a student's development.

Ultimately, as the all-encompassing team concept took over with its "nobody-gets-out-of-anything" position, some of these issues fell into place. The athletic program, for example, changed from a voluntary chance to work off some energy to an essential part of the team effort. All staff members struggled along with everyone else—through baseball games, dormitory hassles, mountain climbing, and how to study for an exam—with their attendant ups and downs, euphoria and depression, goof-offs and confrontations.

The evolution of the roles of staff members, like some of the other methods and techniques applied over the ten summers, was frequently controversial. Chapter 6 examines some of these problems and issues. This evolution, experimentation, and self-examination was, in and of itself, one of the key "parts of the whole."

4

The Program's Effects

THE DATA WE HAVE: "SHORT-TERM" EFFECTS

The six-week summer program of the Student Achievement Institute apparently had some strikingly positive effects for the students within the first year after their return back home. Most of the short-term data were obtained by way of questionnaires (see Appendix E) mailed to students, parents, and staff members approximately seven months after the end of the summer program. About 20 percent of the students had some kind of post-Institute contact with staff members, most through correspondence, a few through face-to-face meetings.

One clear indication of the students' continuing identification with or feeling toward SAI is shown by the fact that for each of the seven years questionnaires were sent, more than 90 percent of the boys (195 out of 215) responded. Parents responded at an even higher percentage (131 out of 140, or 94 percent). These data, coupled with the responses of staff members (35 out of 37) to their questionnaires, provided the primary framework for evaluating the impact of the Institute's program during the students' first post-Institute year.

General Short-Term Effects

Ninety-four percent of the students reported that they observed improvement in their general behavior and attitudes. One hundred percent reported that they could see a positive

55

change in at least one dimension of their life. When asked simply
to "comment" or describe their reactions to the program,
approximately 33 percent chose to speak about the general
overall effects it had on their lives.

Larry:

> On the way home in the car after the Institute, I thought they
> would be asking me all kinds of questions about everything, but
> they didn't. They played it real cool and have ever since. I can
> only remember one time I've been jumped on about doing
> homework. It's been quite a change.
>
> I know I'm doing more and better independent planning.
> For instance, my parents went to Europe for three weeks in
> October. While they were gone, I found that I was organizing
> study time on Saturdays and Sundays. I never would have done
> that before this summer.
>
> I couldn't possibly describe what the Institute did for me.
> I guess maybe because it's so important. I was afraid that, as
> time passed, I would lose a lot of it, what I gained, I mean—
> mostly in self-confidence. But, you know, it's the other way
> around; I've ben able to build on it. It shows not just with my
> family but with everyone. . . . If you hadn't asked me, I wouldn't
> have been able to talk about it. . . . My grades aren't that much
> better yet, but believe me, I am. I would really like to see some
> of the guys again, especially Tom, Alan, and Neil.

And, from others:

> In thinking back to the six weeks I was at the Institute, I cannot
> think of any single incident or experience that, in itself, affected
> me greatly, but as a whole the experience of attending the Insti-
> tute was perhaps one of the most significant experiences of my
> life.

> I'm not so ticked off, I understand my parents, they understand
> me, I am going to college, and I gained twelve pounds.

> I seem to be a helluva lot happier with myself. I'm not as
> nervous or worried as I used to be and I can just feel good
> even if there's nothing to feel good about. Although I was a bit
> skeptical at the close of SAI, I realize now I had no real reason

to be so. You cats have a really great program and I cannot find any suggestions for improvement as I turn over my memory cells. I only hope that soon you will be able to expand your program to make more people's lives a little easier.

Staff members also frequently felt that this general kind of impact was SAI's greatest strength. As one of them commented:

I learned that behavior *actually* changed, and dramatically so, in the six short weks. I've worked with many kids for a whole school year in the once-a-week model and few, if any, achieved as dramatic a transformation of feelings nor gleaned as much self-insight as all seven of our team.

Specific Short-Term Effects

There were also some specific areas in which the Institute seemed to have its greatest short-term effect. For example, 86 percent of the students who responded over the ten years reported that they now had more confidence in their relationships with their peers, 74 percent felt that they were more confident with their parents ("I have become closer to my parents."), and 69 percent felt that they were more confident with their teachers. More than 85 percent felt that the primary positive effect was on their level of self-awareness and self-confidence. From a student:

I learned more about myself in these six weeks than I have known in my life. This has been a great help to me and I feel it wasn't wasted.

From a parent:

The group discussions—the feeling of acceptance of the staff— the sharing of problems with peers and the honesty and direct-ness of the approach. He expressed many times the fact that he had to accept the responsibility for his actions while there. . . . It gave him an increased self-awareness—an ability to look at himself more honestly—increased his interest in discussions and working through a problem rather than covering it up.

All the students seemed to feel that some fairly specific "how-to" ideas emerged from their experience. These two comments are typical:

> Although I was not actually changed, I did see *how* to solve problems. The effect of the Institute is not a dramatic overnight thing. In the future, it will materialize.

> I have a far better "philosophy": I am able to run my own life more effectively. I have cooled down and can accept many things I formerly detested.

The results were significantly more mixed with regard to academic performance. Sixty-eight percent of the students believed that the Institute improved their level of motivation in the academic area. The comments below are a sampling:

> In general, this school year has been a much better year for me. My attitude toward school and my parents has changed for the better. I get along with my parents much better than last year. I seem to be able to do more of what I want because I do more for them without bitching over it like I did last year. I don't sweat school so much, although I do worry about college. I study more but I don't mind it so much. It seems to come a lot easier than last year. I get more things done on time than I did last year and my grades have gone up at least ten points. I believe my whole outlook on life changed toward the end of the summer and, because of this change, my grades improved.

> I got my own motivation rather than my parents'.

> My attitude and my marks have improved. My attitude more than my marks. I grew up.

> The major change is that I can make myself study. No longer am I capable of dreaming up excuses that hold.

While 81 percent of the students reported that their grades had improved within this first year back home, comments from both students and parents seem to indicate that the Institute did not have as significant an effect in terms of specific academic grades as it did in some other areas. One student reported:

I'm not entirely unchangeable, but I no longer feel that I must conform myself to attitudes and characteristics which I admire in other people. I'm me. Acidemically (and spelling wise), I have not changed but I have come to a better view of myself. This defeats the purpose of the Student Achievement Institute, Inc., but for me I appreciate what was done.

About 75 percent of the students and their parents seemed to believe that this was both understandable and acceptable, as reflected in the statement below:

I do not feel that the success of the Institute should be based upon mere better grades. The Institute is valuable to anyone who is having difficulties adjusting with his parents, teachers, or his peers.

It was also an objective of SAI to have a positive impact on staff members. Ninety-seven percent of them reported such an impact with reactions like the following:

Personally, the Institute has made of me a better teacher, more sensitivity, insight, effectiveness generally. Also it has caused, maybe even inspired, me to pursue a further degree in counseling.

The intense involvement with the personal growth of some of the boys plus the professional involvement with some of the staff promoted a lot of motivation and growth on my part. It was very energy-draining—sometimes difficult to maintain the necessary pace—though that is a function of too much intensity rather than lack of helpfulness. It has been very helpful in family counseling sessions and in individual sessions with adolescents in promoting a more directive and involved style, which seems to be a more effective manner with this specific clientele. Working with one of the past students from SAI, seeing him before the summer and now, and the changes that have taken place, makes the effort worthwhile.

Non-Questionnaire Short-Term Data

Staff members obviously found it very difficult to be completely objective (pro or con) immediately following the intensity of a summer session. Short-term information obtained from them concerning the students, however, was generally consistent with—though slightly more conservative than—data obtained from students and parents.

There was literally unanimous agreement that every student "got something." There was also agreement that one or two (depending on the summer) probably "did not get much." The area in which the staff felt SAI was least effective was improvement in grades, both immediate and permanent. They expressed their greatest optimism about its impact on self-confidence and personal development.

Unfortunately (and frustratingly), the staff was unable to agree on why a student was "unreached" and on what characteristics the unreached shared with the others. Most agreed that SAI was less likely to "work" with the boy whose tested I.Q. fell in the average or less-than-average range and who was underachieving relative to *this* potential. The same was true of the students whose emotional problems were most severe and extensive. Beyond that, similarities were difficult to discover. Of the least helped some were hyperaggressive; some were overly passive; some had severe "hang-ups" with authority; some had completely absorbed their parents' rationalizations of their underachievement. Some of the most helped, however, had these same characteristics. For the most part, students seemed to be unreached—just as they seemed to underachieve—for highly individualized reasons.

The few staff members who had much post-Institute exposure to SAI students reported, with only one exception, highly favorable results. Typical is the following comment:

> Incidentally, Bert, who is attending_____High School, is a different young man, and if the rest of our grads are anything like him, we are indeed a success! It is absolutely amazing. His attitude is healthy, positive, energetic, and, behold, achievement-oriented! I have had many occasions to talk with Bert's teachers and his parents and am very pleased to report that the consensus is all optimistic about his future. I really enjoy seeing the expressions on teachers' faces when they mention his name and the obvious changes we are witnessing. . . .

The "exception" was not able to cope with the strains of his former situation.

> It just was not enough; once Jim was faced with all the same old "hassles," he reverted to many, though not all, of his bad habits.

Systematic questionnaire data were not available from non-SAI professionals who had contact with SAI "graduates," but occasionally some feedback was received. A teacher wrote concerning Larry (who had previously been active but only moderately successful in sports) in the November following his SAI summer:

> I've had several contacts with Larry and I understand he is one of the top seniors at_____High School, captain of the lacrosse team, and a key member of the state championship soccer team. I am presently recommending him for Williams. I talked personally with their Director of Admissions and they are very much interested in Larry because of his blossoming this year.

A social worker wrote about the impact the boys had on children with whom they worked during a special project:

> I am writing to thank you for the excellent and helpful evaluations written by the student supervisors during the Student Achievement Institute Summer Program just concluded. Our child care staff here were impressed with the insights that many of these young men seemed to possess, and found the material helpful in our understanding, particularly of the educational needs of the children that were in the program.
>
> I am sorry that I missed you at the critique session we had on July 31. Your wife and other staff persons were very helpful and I think we had a good exchange of ideas and views as well as impressions. There were various significant elements highlighted by the young men: the children's loneliness, the important element of young male people to relate to these children with its big brother and/or father figure association, their ideas and techniques for handling elements of loneliness, need for relationships, and the educational problems they present. Most of us

seem to share the feeling that it was a good, mutually rewarding experience. For my part, I know that the children enjoyed it and certainly my child care staff here noted the children's enthusiasm as the program went along. The point I made at the critique which was shared by members there as well was that the only unfortunate part perhaps is that it only went on for a month rather than perhaps hopefully three months. In line with that, I look for the program to continue and would be very happy to be involved in it with you and your people again next year.

THE DATA WE HAVE: "LONG-TERM" EFFECTS

At the end of both the fifth and the tenth year of the Student Achievement Institute, questionnaires were mailed to all former students, their parents, and all staff members. The number of individuals who could be contacted in this manner decreased, of course, the longer they had been away from the Institute. By the end of the tenth year, for example, 18 percent of the questionnaires were returned by the post office. It was assumed, perhaps incorrectly, that the remainder did, in fact, receive the material. Of this remainder, 40 percent of the parents (total of 82) and 30 percent of the students (62) returned the questionnaires, as did 100 percent of the staff who could be contacted (28 out of 37). The rate of return was highest, not surprisingly, among the most recent "graduates" but, considering the length of time that many had been away from the summer program, the percentages are not bad.

From this longer term perspective, as compared with the perspective of only seven months after the summer experience, the students and their parents expressed (1) a continuing sense of positiveness from an overall point of view, (2) a similar positive feeling about certain specific aspects of the program, but quite mixed perceptions of its impact in certain other areas, and (3) a heightened awareness of some missing components.

(For purposes of *statistical* analysis, respondents to the ten-year questionnaire who participated in SAI during the first five years are eliminated. This avoids the potential problem of anonymous duplicate five-year and ten-year answers. It also, if anything, makes the percentages less positive, since the preponderance of those who were eliminated were highly positive.)

General Long-Term Effects

On the Rating Scale of the five-year and ten-year questionnaires, 83 percent of the students who responded indicated that the experience for them was either "valuable" or "very valuable." Seventy-one percent of the parents gave these same ratings. Only 2 percent of the students described the experience as "not valuable," a reaction given explicitly by 4 percent of the parents but implicitly by approximately another 2 percent.

In more than 95 percent of the cases, a given student and his parents ranked eight out of nine specific effects of the program in exactly the same order (for example, agreeing that the boy received most in the area of confidence-building and least in the area of peer relationships). The exception concerned the relationship between parents and son, with the boys tending to rate SAI's contribution low and the parents high. One boy put it this way:

> The Institute made me realize that I wasn't "over the hill," that I could be a success, and gave me the opportunity to get a new grip on myself, experiment, and "reach out." It gave me a new confidence and I realized that there were many others who had problems too. My dad, whom I feel had a great deal to do with my lack of confidence in myself, had not changed *his* habits (nor was he about to). I found long exposure at home a detriment to my improvement and my new confidence in self aggravated his domination.

It might be mentioned here that the perceptions of students and those of parents were consistently similar through all parts of the long-term questionnaires. Parents and students generally perceived the same *kinds* of changes, but the parents were somewhat more critical (or perhaps realistic) in assessing the *degree* of change which occurred. In only about 6 percent of the replies

received from both a boy and his parents did a significant difference exist between their assessments (for example, on the Rating
Scale, a boy rating the experience above the midpoint of the
scale and the parent rating it below the midpoint).

The students' one-word descriptions of SAI were very positive. About 25 percent of them used words such as *fantastic,
amazing, exceptional,* and *enriching.* Another 25 percent described
it as *useful, helpful,* or *worthwhile.* Other words included *ener-
getic, an experience, awareness,* and *fun.* Students who, in open-
ended parts of the questionnaire, were most critical (about 12
percent) still used the word *interesting.* One described it as a
"waste of time" but then went on to qualify that reaction by
saying that he expected dramatic short-term improvement and
discovered that the changes which occurred in him were more
long-term in coming.

The majority of parents viewed SAI extremely positively.
They used words like *godsend, many thanks, excellent,* and
helpful to describe their reactions. Others (four percent), however,
said the Institute was not effective, no help at all, and incomplete.
One parent indicated that, if anything, the Institute's contribution was very negative and "delayed proper treatment." Below
are a cross-section of students' comments:

> The advantages that I obtained really took effect long after I
> left SAI or I should say I didn't utilize and take advantage of
> them.

> SAI contributed much to my life, most strongly soon after the
> summer. SAI I feel helped me to realize that I too am a con-
> tributing and valuable person, unique, too. I began to realize
> my potential and I was genuinely satisfied with what I saw. I
> saw many possibilities for my life and my outlook is much
> brighter.

> It has been quite some time since I attended SAI, and it is hard
> to attribute specific things which have taken place to one or
> more benefits received at SAI. At the time I entered SAI, *I
> needed it,* and the values I received were innumerable. I would
> *highly* recommend it to anyone who is in a situation similar to
> the one I was in.

I found out that I was being negative—I knew what I couldn't do or didn't want to be—now I am thinking and acting in a more positive manner and am doing much better. It really didn't help me academically that much; I never managed to motivate myself while in college—no fault of the program, however.

From the parents:

If SAI had not become available for him when it did, as a junior in high school, I am sure he would have dropped out.

I want you to know how very much we truly appreciate all you have done for Herbert. Before taking your training, he could not and would not sit down and talk things out; if something bothered him he went into his shell or burst apart, so to speak, with frustration. Now, he handles it and discusses it (after the initial burst) quite calmly and reaches his decision with common sense. Undoubtedly we parents learned to "give" more, from the deeper understanding you helped us to reach. And our guidelines are not as rigid as before.

I am grateful that my son had the experience of attending SAI. Apart from scholastic achievement, he has matured into a fine, responsible young man. He entered SAI with many good attitudes and others not so good; SAI seems to have magnified the positive and minimized the negative.

Larry's parents, four and a half years later, described his SAI summer as a "lifesaver":

It gave him self-confidence, a realistic self-image. It enabled him to function more effectively at school, at home, on his job—had changed his role from possibly a casualty of life to a "winner." Made my wife and me better parents—improved our understanding and interaction of and with each other. Helped us face the deeper issues of marriage and family life instead of getting hung up on surface matters. Our whole family is the better for SAI.

These parental comments seem particularly noteworthy in light of the staff's perennial dissatisfaction with their efforts to help parents directly.

Specific Long-Term Effects

As for the Institute's long-run impact in specific areas, students and parents alike agreed that its most positive contributions were in terms of students' increased self-awareness (97 percent of students, 96 percent of parents), their positive emotional adjustment (90 percent of students, 94 percent of parents), and to a somewhat lesser degree, their improved relationships with peers and teachers (76 percent of students, 93 percent of parents). Students who were less positive in their assessment tended to emphasize their discovery that personal change was inevitably a long, slow process, so that, while they felt somewhat frustrated with their summer experience initially, they later came to perceive it as successful.

In the long-term data as in the short-term, students and their parents agreed in general that a less significant contribution was made in the areas of vocational effectiveness, extracurricular effectiveness and, to some degree, academic effectiveness—although the data were very mixed. One boy described his experience as a "complete success" and went on to say:

> I had done extremely bad in school until I attended SAI. I flunked three out of five subjects my sophomore year in high school. SAI was a complete success, not necessarily in the immediate future (after that summer), but in the long run. My junior year (following SAI summer) in high school I went back to prep school and did not do too well so I went back to public school and decided to do some work and made the honor roll three out of four times. I now have a 2.96 grade average out of community college.

Another found very little value in terms of academic impact:

> The contribution of SAI was not valuable so much in terms of vocational or academic success as in regard to personal insight, acceptance, and ability to relate effectively to people and situations. I am still not particularly ambitious.

The overwhelming majority of students and parents seemed in retrospect to accept this mixed result quite willingly. From a student:

> There was no academic change. No change, unless negative, in my work habits—but I don't attribute it to SAI. The most valuable changes came as personal changes. After SAI I gradually became more and more aware of and more in contact with my feelings, therefore I had a big social change, a big change in attitudes toward people and that was about as big a change I think I could've handled at that time.

From a parent:

> As a matter of information, Chris is still something less than a real achiever in scholastics, athletics, and other related accepted pursuits for his years. On the other hand, he is continuing to pursue his natural bent which is in the field of manual skills. More important, he has become a pretty wholesome person, a pleasure to live with, and a human being who will probably recognize his true potential to a greater degree than I, despite my apparent material success. In other words, I think SAI did him a lot of good. It also helped his parents to allow him more freedom to go his own way.
>
> In terms of self-awareness and emotional adjustment, I believe my son benefited enormously. To me nothing was then—or is now—more important. I believe the supportive assistance he received then will benefit him for the rest of his life. It did not help him academically at all and in no way did it really help him accept authority. It gave both my son and myself some perspective. As a result of SAI we were able to "cool it," to take a fresh look at each other. Both of us relaxed previously rigid positions to a degree that we came to respect each other's lifestyles even though they are very different. We realized that fundamentally we share the same values and are excellent "friends" today.

Objective academic data were available for only about 20 percent of the alumni in the post-Institute years. The summer experience seemed to have a curvilinear impact on the grades of this group. Typically, they returned home with a vigor which led to an initial upsurge in academic performance. Then, five or six months after leaving the Institute, it was not uncommon for this performance to deteriorate. Finally, for approximately 60 percent of the students, academic grades began to improve again. From a parent:

> SAI got through to him and convinced him or led him to his own conviction on the relevance and importance of effort and achievement in his life. He started off strong in college but, after an initial success, relapsed to older ways. I wish the conviction and effort could have stayed with him more consistently. The curve did turn up again, however, and as of today in his senior year at college both effort, current results, and a mature sense of direction in life are all very, very good.

The staff seemed to respond to the long-term questionnaire "from a cloud." On the Rating Scale, 100 percent rated the experience as valuable or very valuable to them personally. In six of eight specific areas within that overall experience, they also rated SAI's contribution as positive or very positive: in overall professional competence, effectiveness with adolescents, ideas for implementation, insight into individual adolescents, understanding of underachievement, and their own personal growth. The two areas in which SAI's impact was less than good were research endeavors and specific usable techniques.

All of the one-word characterizations by the staff were also on the positive side: effective, change, challenging, concentrated, useful, enjoyable, exciting, super, fantastic, and so on.

Missing Components

As for features which the Institute lacked, the "wish" most frequently expressed by students, parents, and staff on the long-term questionnaires was for some kind of a follow-up. From a student:

> I feel that the value of SAI would be greatly enhanced by a follow-up program on an advanced (college) level . . . as little as one weekend every two or three months would greatly help in *retaining* high motivation.

From a parent:

> The work you begin is of great value. Ed did very well through the fall term; but the gradual grinding, with some emphasis on his stupidity in language, slowly but surely disintegrated his newfound confidence and effort. The follow-up in the schools the boys returned to would greatly enhance your program.

From two staff members:

> I concluded for the first time that underachievers require an interruption of their regular schooling and need, instead, a full time SAI experience for a year or more.

> SAI tries to do too much in too short a time; however, the experience is so intense that I doubt many staff members could take it much longer.

DATA WE WISH WE HAD

There was a continuing struggle within the SAI community as to just how "scientific" and research-oriented the Institute should be. The incorporators viewed research as a major objective. During the massive self-analysis at the end of five years, a substantial number of suggestions were made to the effect that the Institute needed to develop a more sophisticated base of research and data which could, in turn, lead to a more scientific evaluation of its programs and efforts.

Counterbalancing these concerns were several factors. First, there was the strong conviction of staff members that the Institute was providing a genuine service to a particular group of boys and that this should be the first priority. Second, the staff members became deeply involved each summer in helping the students who were present—even if those staff members had originally been hired to devote some time to research. Third, funding problems always made it necessary to make choices, and the decision always went in the direction of providing direct services. Fourth, staff members concluded that data could be provided to parents and educators on the basis of the clinical experiences which were occurring—and, it was hoped, these data would be helpful to people concerned with the problem of underachievement, including those interested in conducting research into some of the specific observations made during the Institute's program.

At the conclusion of the tenth summer program, it became clear that there were a good many data "we wished we had"—irrespective of the question of whether the Institute could have or should have gathered those data. Such data would have been helpful in evaluating more completely the impact of the Institute's efforts.

Clearly, it would be helpful to have more follow-up data on students who participated in the Institute, especially in the form of hard data such as academic grades achieved, how far the students ultimately went academically, and so on. Evaluations made by teachers of the performance of the students would add an important perspective, as would input from other professionals working with them. It would be good to know more about whether staff recommendations were acted upon or rejected, post-SAI. For example, how many students actually continued psychotherapy? For how long? With what results? More opportunity for SAI staff members to keep in touch with the students over a period of several years could have been a highly provocative source of information.

Another frequently mentioned source of data, particularly within the context of a scientific model, would have been the use of a control group. While obviously a very complex undertaking, important insights would have been gained by identifying a group of students with backgrounds, intellectual abilities, academic performances, and so on, that were comparable to the students participating in the Institute's program. It would then be possible to compare the later performance of this group who did not have the SAI experience with the SAI students, and thus ascertain the nature of the impact of SAI.

Another kind of "data we wish we had" is a series of interviews with SAI students and their parents based on their responses to the follow-up questionnaires. This would obviously permit a more in-depth elaboration and understanding of a student's or a parent's statement that "my life is different" or "I am more self-confident" or "his academic performance didn't change."

Another kind of missing data would describe the day-to-day processes involved in the summer program. In retrospect, it is clear that it would be advantageous to have transcripts of staff members' written logs, and even of the provocative kinds of informal discussions which occurred in tents on camping trips or on the steps of the dorm. There would be clear value in having more in-depth ongoing data following a particular student's feelings and attitudes as he went through the summer experience.

It frequently occurred to staff members that although a considerable amount of experimentation with various techniques was occurring during the summer, very little was being recorded concerning the impact of these different kinds of techniques. There would be value, for example, in having evidence on the effects of different types of therapeutic approaches consistently maintained throughout the summer.

One doctoral student did use the Institute to study the relationship between depression and underachievement. While this particular investigation did not translate readily into daily work with underachieving teenagers, it would have been worthwhile to encourage more of this kind of research effort which caused little interference in the Institute's day-to-day operations.

Finally, we wish we had more consistently usable demographic data. For example, while we know that only about 5 percent of the students came from truly low-income families and that about 75 percent came from high-income families, we do not know the specific income distribution. Other background information of this nature would be very useful.

5

What
We Have Learned

It was tempting for the staff of the Student Achievement Institute to assume they were discovering brilliant new insights into the process of underachievement. A more modest assessment, however, indicated that one of the Institute's primary contributions was a repeated reinforcement and elaboration of already hypothesized notions. During the Institute's ten-year existence, a wealth of new books, research papers, and forums were adding similar reinforcements and shedding new insights. (See the Annotated Bibliography in Appendix F.)

During this same period of time, some educators began questioning the value of the term "underachievement," suggesting, for example, that underachievement might instead be viewed as *overprediction* of potential or ability. The SAI staff remained convinced, however, that underachievement was a psychologically-educationally valid concept, in part because of the strong clinical impression of unrealized potential. It was also clear that too much had been subsumed under the heading of underachievement, including the difficulties of individuals with serious emotional disturbance, with brain injury, or with experiences of substantial cultural deprivation (see Appendix G). SAI's intended focus was toward those individuals whose academic underachievement was the "primary symptom," without severe emotional disturbance or neurological damage in the classic sense. Given this definition, the SAI program seemed to confirm or reinforce a series of generalizations concerning (1) the underachieving process, (2) the underachiever, and (3) parental-educational-psychological work with the underachiever.

THE UNDERACHIEVING PROCESS

During the ten years of SAI summer programs, there was repeated reinforcement of the idea that underachievement, for any particular person, is a unique and individualized experience. Different people underachieve for different reasons and in different ways. While utilizing basic research from such areas as early learning and motivation, the staff learned to let the data and the explanations unfold from each student and his family. Just as psychologists have discovered that there are innumerable and sometimes surprising motives for success, there appear to be an unlimited number of causes for not succeeding.

There was simultaneous reconfirmation of the notion that the underachiever's parents and teachers could, usually unwittingly, contribute to or magnify the problem. Staff members observed students trying to equal or surpass a father "with seven degrees" or struggling to communicate with a mother who said she "didn't realize a boy baby needed to be told he was loved." In a number of instances, adult expectations were impossibly high and, in other instances, the adults had clearly given up. It was also ironically clear that often the profound sense of frustration and stress felt by the parents perpetuated a vicious circle for all concerned, with "uptight" parents stimulating "uptight" kids. (See "A Brief Note to Parents of Underachieving Students" at the end of this chapter.) Other key adults in the student's environment, including the educational setting, were often apparently tempted to view his behavior in fairly superficial terms—what some staff members came to call the "he-could-if-he-wanted-to" phenomenon.

The SAI experience consistently confirmed the theory that underachievement is usually a generalized and chronic form of behavior. The Institute was clearly not dealing with something that began yesterday or last year. With rare exceptions, examination of elementary school records and teacher comments revealed that the child was underproducing in relation to measured capacity even then. Similarly, with an overwhelming majority of SAI students, the boy underachieved in virtually all aspects of his life. In contrast to outward appearances, he typically underachieved academically, socially, athletically, as well as in his nonschool activities.

The Institute obtained reinforcement also for the observation that underachievement can range in form from a relatively passive, "I won't make the effort" to a very active, "I refuse to achieve"—the latter frequently referred to as "antiachievement." In the latter case, students with exceptionally high intellectual abilities had to work unusually hard and dynamically to fail in school.

UNDERACHIEVERS

Given the variety of causes and forms of underachievement, the staff became wary of making general comments about the psychological makeup of a "typical" underachiever. Nevertheless, certain kinds of psychological characteristics, most of which had previously been identified in the literature, were common among the students at the Institute. The six perspectives utilized in the Psychological Studies provide a format for organizing these generalizations.

Intellectual Characteristics

The underachiever at SAI simply did not effectively apply his demonstrably strong intellectual resources. Some were lopsided in the kinds of abilities they possessed—strong nonverbally but weak verbally, for example. Because of the typical school's emphasis on repeating courses that are failed instead of capitalizing on areas of success, this student rarely discovered or exploited his strengths. Others became caught up in, and frustrated by, a system geared to the average student with an emphasis on the concrete and the structured. Almost all took a highly formalistic and inhibited approach to problem solving, at the expense of creativity and imagination. Both the breadth and the depth of their attack on problems were highly restricted.

Emotional Characteristics

The self-esteem of the student was significantly impaired, despite frequent facades which suggested the contrary. The underproducing male adolescents at the Institute basically had a very low opinion of themselves and a very inaccurate self-concept. They had come to expect failure. As a result, they were extremely anxious in almost all learning situations.

They did demonstrate a considerable degree of diversity (and some might say creativity) in dealing with these kinds of feelings. Some took a low-risk, "nothing-ventured-nothing-lost" approach to life; others were more inclined to take a high-risk, "hopeless-long-shot" kind of approach. Both styles seemed to provide a greater sense of security and an easier justification for failure than any attempt to master systematically something that the boy believed he couldn't handle. It was quite common to rationalize difficulties, rather than to confront them head-on.

The underachiever typically handled his hostilities very poorly, not uncommonly turning them inward. One staff member mirrored to his team the reaction of his four-year-old son angrily responding to parental discipline with, "I'm not even going to learn my letters!" "Getting" someone else by getting himself— "I'll show you, *I* won't learn," or "I'll get me"—was a very common vehicle used by the underachieving students in expressing their anger. The passive, indirect expression of aggressiveness —like stubbornness and resistance—was prevalent.

They also had more than a little trouble handling authority relationships—on both the giving and the receiving ends. Almost all had, at best, very mixed feelings about key adults in their world—parents, teachers, counselors, and so on. They would cope with these feelings and relationships in wide-ranging but rarely maturely effective ways. Active resistance and passive compliance were common, and one of the students' prevailing struggles was to learn how to "take" and interact with the staff. Similarly, as possessors of authority, almost all found leadership roles to be discomforting.

These students were, additionally, deficient in their capacity to delay gratification. "Fun and games" rather than the "pain and suffering" of study was prevalent. One staff member reported that on an eight-hour automobile trip the initial gaiety of the departure was immediately followed with a request for a stop for food. When the request was denied and the boys were asked to wait, the mood dramatically changed. The adults became the depriving "heavies" and hostile sparks flew. The students' need for immediate satisfaction seemed to interfere severely with their ability to persist and to achieve. If they couldn't have a good grade *right now,* then ongoing perseverance "wasn't worth the hassle."

Motivational Characteristics

Student underachievers appeared to be strongly motivated by a pair of conflicting unconscious psychological needs that are frequently found in other adolescents: the need to depend or rely on others and the need to be independent. The underachiever, with his expectations of failure, was especially fearful of going out on his own and found his helplessness effective in attracting support and attention from other people. Yet, at the same time, he often aggressively asserted his independence from adults, frequently through an intense involvement with (and suscepti- bility to) his peer group.

The students also exhibited a distinct and dynamic driving need to build up some sense of self-respect and pride. Noteworthy was their emphasis on "looking good" in their own eyes rather than on risking any real commitment to a task. Often, then, they would put on the self-deceptive appearance of effort without truly pursuing an end result.

In a related fashion, it also seemed clear that the under-achiever was rarely goal-oriented or future-oriented in his motivation. Lack of self-confidence seemed to hold him back from working toward either short-range or long-range goals.

Insight

Many underachieving students, with their high intelligence, possessed excellent potential for insight into themselves or other people, but they typically did not apply it. They had never really looked at their own needs and feelings and had worked hard to avoid examining the self-defeating nature of their approach to life. They also rarely understood the feelings and motivations of others or the impact they themselves had on others. They preferred to assume little personal responsibility for any outcome—especially failure—and avoided feedback on their performance. In effect, they cut themselves off from self-defining experiences.

Skill in Human Relations

Within the context of the Institute, the generalized nature of underachievement appeared to be clearly confirmed in the students' interpersonal skills. Their skills were at best superficial, frequently involving "big talk" but little ability to relate in a close or genuine way with others. On one excursion off campus, the bus of SAI students ended up being parked side by side with a busload of teenage girls. A considerable number of promises, threats, and plans floated from the SAI bus—until they were given permission to leave the bus. The only reaction was a deathly silence.

Academic Skills

In a word, they usually had none. A substantial amount of time had typically been spent with them in attempts to develop academic skills, but they came to the Institute with poor study habits, an inability to concentrate, generally low reading skills, and little understanding of the techniques of learning and studying.

PARENTAL-EDUCATIONAL-PSYCHOLOGICAL WORK
WITH THE UNDERACHIEVER

The SAI experience produced evidence supporting a number of ways in which parents, educators, and other concerned individuals could potentially help the underachieving teenager.

It appeared quite clear that the problem of underachievement required a "total person solution," that is, an experience impactful enough to affect the student's self-concept so that using his abilities could become a source of satisfaction. More superficial treatments, like appealing to reason, bullying, or shaming, just did not seem to work. Nor did an isolated, single-thrust kind of approach seem sufficient, be it tutoring *or* psychotherapy *or* taking a different academic program. The staff agreed that it was the total milieu and gestalt of the Institute which had the ultimate impact, with every part of the boy's daily life used to provide influences in the direction of self-understanding and increased personal achievement. Undoubtedly, a significant portion of this impact occurred simply because a dramatic change or some kind—any kind—of action was happening. But, again, a "total" program seemed essential.

At the same time, it appeared that the ability to achieve and the feeling of achievement in one activity or area of life could be transferred to other areas. As one academic counselor put it:

I began to feel that it didn't make too much difference how or in what area—athletic, academic, extracurricular, or psychological—a student was first moved, as long as he was indeed moved. It seemed that a student's progress in any one of these areas was often a step toward a more pervasive general improvement, adjustment, and even academic achievement on a realistic scale. Progress in one area was almost always reflected eventually in another area. The grouping of students into teams was an excellent way of enhancing this motivational cross-fertilization. A boy who was inspired to compete on the basketball floor was often better able to accept, even welcome, scholastic competition.

Some observers, particularly parents for whom the proof of the pudding is an immediately better academic performance, cannot accept the compromise which is temporarily inherent in this approach. It seems to me that these objectors cannot see far enough ahead. Once an underachiever's inertia is broken, movement begins with interest, is hastened by enthusiasm, and eventually leads to achievement at a higher level. In this program, we are seldom working with lopsided students who have at least one area of achievement to boast. The students we have seen have been underachievers in almost every area of their lives, even in the way they waste time.

There seemed to be strong evidence that the student was helped when some way was found for him to achieve.

The individual psychotherapy conducted with each of the students during the SAI program was, to the surprise of most of the staff, mentioned by the students most often as the single most important positive contribution to them. As compared with the transient "patchwork treatment" most of them had undergone previously, the intense and focused nature of the psychotherapy sessions seemed to be of value, regardless of the theoretical perspective of the therapist. As a result of this, most staff members found themselves urging psychotherapy for underachievers, even when they could not have the benefit of an environment like SAI. However, they recognized that it might not have much impact on academic performance. It was hard to make up for years of massive frustration and little formal learning. Simultaneous academic tutoring which was psychotherapeutically oriented was sometimes found to be of assistance.

With these general observations as a backdrop, a number of more specific guidelines emerged from the experience of the Student Achievement Institute, guidelines which appeared to help the staff create the overall "milieu."

1. *Develop a good understanding of the total student.* Before any real progress could be made, it was necessary, for example, to discover his real needs, to understand the nature of his fears, and to observe the modes of adjustment he was using.

2. *Help him obtain increased self-understanding.* Change in behavior was often related to the development of insight into the student's own feelings, the self-defeating nature of his adjust-

ment, and other aspects of his psychological makeup. For example, usable nonjudgmental feedback helped.

3. *Reduce his anxiety.* Although some tension could be helpful in effecting change, the underachiever's doubts and fears were typically so extensive that he was more or less immobilized by anxiety. Books or professionally conducted training sessions that facilitated relaxation were frequently utilized.

4. *Get him involved in his own program of self-improvement.* The underachiever needed help in establishing meaningful goals for himself—goals based on his strengths, not on the older generation's interests. Beyond that, he had to get into action, receiving lots of support along the way.

5. *Help him, especially initially, to create short-range goals.* The object was to have success likely, so the goals had to be reachable, realistic, and within reasonable expectations. Example: Aim for study-time goals that were realistic for *him*—this-week's-assignment goals rather than A-for-the-course goals.

6. *See that the goals are related to observable and measurable behavior changes.* The underachiever needed to see results that he could sink his teeth into. Quantifying a goal made it possible for him to know when he had succeeded.

7. *Emphasize successes rather than failures.* Gradually, in small doses, increasingly demanding goals could be set *after* initial successes.

8. *Reward the positive—with praise or whatever—rather than punishing the negative.*

9. *See that the student receives immediate feedback concerning his progress.* The longer the lag, the weaker the connection between what he did and what happened as a result.

10. *Help him fully appreciate the principle of cause and effect.* The underachiever seldom believed that he could control outcomes or that, for example, hard work really could get results.

11. *Encourage a spirit of competition, primarily of self-competition.* The underachiever needed to "stretch himself," keeping a record of his own improvement.

12. *Encourage experimentation, imagination, spontaneity,*

and learning by doing. This, of course, implied enough flexibility so that some "goofs" could be absorbed. It implied letting the student try that crazy study schedule—as long as it could be evaluated objectively.

13. *Encourage activities outside the academic area.* The traditional way of limiting outside activities for underperforming students seemed to ignore the principle that success in one area tended to lead to success in others. The student who wasn't involved in something didn't have a chance to succeed.

14. *Provide him with an adult who will support him and give personal tutorial assistance.* The underachieving adolescent needed to feel there was someone significant who was interested in him and could be depended upon to help him, especially an "authority figure" outside the home.

15. *Check results so as to keep alert for any need for a change in approach.*

16. *Encompass all of these guidelines with a policy of constant attention to the underachiever's environment.* With critical awareness, it was often possible to find apparently insignificant factors that actually were having an important, direct influence on his performance. Often a direct question to the student brought out useful data here.

In the Institute's contacts with the parents of underachievers, it became clear that their particularly difficult situation should be addressed very directly. The frustration and anger they felt in their attempts to relate to their son were much more intense than anything experienced by his teachers and counselors. Their usual berating, cajoling, lecturing, etc., was understandable but almost always nonproductive. The general guidelines listed above seemed helpful to them; psychotherapy for the student and/or his family might well be a worthwhile investment; and serious reading (see Appendix F) could stimulate substantial growth. Still, some parental soul-searching seemed warranted.

The following commentary was written by Milton Kornrich, SAI veteran psychologist, as a result of work with parents.

A BRIEF NOTE TO PARENTS OF
UNDERACHIEVING STUDENTS

Has all your yelling, worrying, punishing, and promising significantly altered his (her) achievement? Invariably, of course, the answer is no. So why *continue* with a no pay-off course? (On some level, underachievement is masochistic, as is the parental response. Both lead nowhere.) Next in this quite predictable sequence is, "Well, okay, let's say we lay off; won't he think we don't care anymore?" Helping the parents to lay off is a major task, and then of course the therapist sets himself up for more negative reactions, when the parents next observe, "See, we followed your advice; never talked about school, never pressured, never checked up on homework or exams, and after six months, he's still failing." Nevertheless, I persist, with two goals in mind: (1) I want parental blood pressure to decrease—for *their* sake; and (2) I want the student to be under less pressure and to disarm him of the phony-baloney excuse of blaming his parents for *his* underachievement. In short, I want to see what *he* does and does not do with respect to school work.

Why, as parents, are you so overconcerned about underachievement? Namely, does one or both parents "push" achievement because they want the child to be *like* or *unlike* them? While the overwhelming majority of parents want their youngster to achieve, sometimes, because of their needs, it is as if they *demand* the "gift" of achievement. Parents who are educators or highly successful business people often appear to be the most "threatened" when one of their children underachieves. For these well-educated, ambitious, usually successful people, underachievement is often perceived as defiance, personal rebuff. (Sometimes it is.)

While I doubt the following question will earn popularity among parents, I believe it is rational and helps hold on to sanity: Is underachievement always bad? Academic underachievement (defined as a significant discrepancy between potential and actual performance) is not a catastrophe, a disaster. Yes, it is something meriting concern and investigation early in the student's academic career. If the etiology is not organic (i.e., reflecting central nervous system dysfunctioning), then psychotherapy and/or educational tutoring and parental counseling are appropriate and have a chance. If, in some instances, the youngster truly rejects academic achievement as a *value* to be endorsed, then the youngster ought not endure the onslaught of parents and educators who endorse the value of achievement. Back off, and perhaps at least compliment yourself for raising an independent thinker—yes, this may be one of the positives in a situation that you find disturbing. Not everyone wants to be "successful" (as defined by you) or formally educated. To underachieve is neither a sin, crime, nor necessarily a rejection of parental standards. In some instances, it is indeed a nonneurotic choice, whether we like it or not.

Finally, is your child underachieving? It is blatantly clear that occasionally parents falsely label their child an underachiever. Less occasionally, but it definitely happens, parents or teachers fail to see that a youngster is underachieving. On both counts, you're dealing with an emotional issue—your own as well as his.

6

Problems
and Unresolved Issues

> I cannot accept the idea that we have been as successful
> as we can be or know what we should about the problem.
> How can we *better* lead a boy to have *more* confidence in
> himself, more pride, to better overcome his natural inertia,
> to develop success-producing habits, to deal with his envi-
> ronment, etc.? Has our present program provided all the
> answers? It has provided some, but it seems to me that we
> have gone only about half way.
> —SAI ACADEMIC COUNSELOR

> I guess achievement is really a process, isn't it?
> —LARRY (THREE MONTHS POST-SAI)

Because of the deliberately experimental and intensely self-
evaluative nature of the program, there frequently was an acute
sensitivity to what *wasn't working* and what had *not yet* been
done. Some problems were clearly problems; that is, a number
of actions were taken in an attempt to deal with them but the
problems remained. Other problems took on the form of unresolved issues; that is, the questions were raised but, by their
very nature, answers were not readily available. In both cases,
whether labeled a "problem" or an "unresolved issue," further
experimentation and conceptualization were clearly needed.

PROBLEMS

The "Unreached" Students

While available data and staff observations indicate that
almost all students got "something" from their SAI experience,
there were some who, from the point of view of almost all concerned, did not significantly benefit from the program. In spite
of careful advance screening, frequent staff conferences, and
considerable flexibility in designing personalized experiences,
there were instances in which staff members, the student himself,
and his parents agreed that the program didn't "take." The
problem was compounded for the boy by the fact that he was
experiencing an additional "failure." Efforts on the part of staff
members to at least minimize his perception of failure met with
only mixed results. The problem was further compounded by
the fact that there did not seem to be consistent commonalities
among these students.

There are several aspects to the problem. First, there is the
possibility that better selection procedures could have kept these
students from being accepted into the Institute, thereby pre-
venting this particular failure. Second, there is the question of
designing situations so that these individuals, even if admitted,
cannot fail—so that even they will change their reactions to
stimuli that would ordinarily have triggered just another defeat.
Third, the task remains of discovering creative alternatives to
help "turn on" the boy who is not helped by the SAI approach.

"Back Home"

There has been substantial experimentation in attempts to
help individuals transfer a learning experience in one situation
to another situation. The problem remains, however, that
students in a program such as the Student Achievement Institute
may learn new attitudes and skills there and then return to the
environment in which the old attitudes were originally learned.

Sometimes, after leaving SAI, students entered another new environment, such as a different private school. This gave them a chance to carry over their new approaches into situations that were not associated with old habits and self-defeating vicious circles. But it avoided the real issue, which is presented by returning to the original environment. A good number of students who went back home did succeed in maintaining the momentum toward achievement that started rolling at the Institute, as the data reported in chapter 4 indicate. Efforts to include the parents in helping the student make this transition appeared useful, just as family therapy has frequently been found to be an alternative superior to individual psychotherapy. The SAI staff found it difficult, however, to arrange enough contact with the parents so that they could accept and prepare themselves for the necessary changes in attitudes and behavior. The problem of a student's return back home remained a problem—both in enabling him to apply his new skills outside of the SAI milieu *and* in impacting and changing his old environment to make the transition easier for him and more healthful for all involved.

Academic Skill Development

Many students and most parents expected the Student Achievement Institute to provide very specific training with regard to academic skills. In general, however, staff members found it much harder to develop these kinds of skills than had been assumed. Most of them were dissatisfied with available instruments for assessing the boys' weaknesses and relied more on direct observation of their study and avoidance-of-study skills. Some books, some individual tutoring, some practice sessions, and some relaxation therapy seemed to help. But staff members tended to see this skill development as a lesser priority than broader based psychological development. Partly as a result of their bias, SAI had greater impact on general personal development than it did on academic development.

Psychosocial Development

That is, girls. As might be expected, the all-male student population was troubled about girls. It was found that contrary to the boasts of the boys the typical underachiever did not have well-developed social skills interacting with girls. Nevertheless, girls in the immediate vicinity were often drawn to the campus by the existence of the Institute. Frequent though somewhat sporadic attempts were made by the staff to organize social activities. Other attempts were made to encourage student contact with women associated with the Institute, including wives of staff members. There was, of course, much discussion of this universal adolescent concern in individual and group therapy sessions and in informal counseling situations. The Student Achievement Institute did not, however, successfully implement an ongoing model or method for dealing with this "problem" or encouraging this kind of development.

The Milieu within the Milieu

Open-systems theories clearly point out the way in which any community is a part of a bigger community. The community of the Student Achievement Institute was a part of a broader community which included the teachers of the academic courses, members of the campus staff, other summer school students, and, of course, the community at large. While students were deliberately placed in academic courses where they would be exposed to the "real world"—that is, teachers who were not part of SAI's staff—frustrating problems did arise because the Institute was unable to elicit the complete understanding and support of non-SAI personnel. While some staff members argued that this was exactly the kind of situation with which the boys needed to learn to cope, others believed that much more could be accomplished if everyone was working together more effectively.

The Toll of Intensity

Although the summer program was deliberately intense, there were distinct costs to that intensity. The physical demands were unusually heavy, particularly for staff members. For both students and staff, reprieves and escapes were hard to come by. When weekend absences were permitted for either staff mmbers or students, it was difficult to rebuild momentum quickly—a real problem in view of the relatively short duration of the program.

Role Conflict and Ambiguity

Staff members were simultaneously placed in the roles of disciplinarian, counselor, coach, surrogate parent, friend, colleague, professional, researcher, and so on. While almost all professionals working with adolescents find themselves in similar kinds of situations, the combination of this diversity with the program's intensity seemed to compound the problem for the SAI staff. There simply were no other adults in the environment to play complementary roles. Furthermore, because staff members became totally involved, most were uncomfortable with the idea of abiding by the most obvious professional distinctions—for example, educator or psychologist. While some attempts were made to define roles so that distinct responsibilities could exist, most of them met resistance from the staff members themselves. Typically, therefore, a multitude of sometimes conflicting roles was required of all of them. From a psychologist's report:

> *Least valuable* contribution to last summer: staff identification with group to such an extent that objectivity, fair play, and sportsmanship are no longer part of a staff member's behavior. This must be avoided at all costs. No staff member doing this should be rehired. This is nondebatable.

Is it best for the psychologist to act clearly as psychotherapist and the educator to act as an educational counselor? Should psychological input be provided on a consultative basis rather than an active-involvement basis (which would, among other things, reduce the cost)? Is there a need for one of the two professionals to serve as the head of the team and, if so, is this logically the academic person? It may be that the Student Achievement Institute did not always make the best use of the differing skills and backgrounds of these two groups of professionals; yet, as described in chapter 3, this role ambiguity had distinct advantages. It multiplied the opportunities for both psychologist and academic counselor to influence the boy's development far beyond what would be possible in their formal sessions with him. And by avoiding fragmentation of the program, it tended to enhance the unified, one-purpose nature of the Institute.

Freedom versus Discipline

One dilemma which had to be resolved in order for staff roles to jell was that of freedom versus discipline. On the one hand, there was a feeling, in recognition of the boys' almost universal conflict with authority, that as far as possible they should be led and encouraged rather than required to do anything beyond the basic academic and psychotherapeutic activities. On the other hand, there was the importance of getting the boy deeply involved as early as possible in the short six weeks available so that the cumulative effect of many small achievements could begin. Many SAI students had already developed an adjustment pattern of avoiding involvement in anything, which meant a delay before they would voluntarily expose themselves to opportunities for change. Perhaps they had to be thrown bodily into the stream of activities.

Another question contained in the freedom versus discipline dilemma was how to deal with infractions of dormitory rules and the like. Some of the psychologists felt that for them to be identified with disciplinary action would interfere with the course of therapy and that, therefore, such matters should be in the hands of the academic counselors. There was another viewpoint, however, as expressed by one psychologist:

> I feel it is necessary for the psychologists to be present and participate in all of the activities of SAI. There also seems to be good theoretical justification for this: We are parental surrogates. We confront these kids with the same kinds of authority dilemmas as do their parents. We are there so that the students can "work through" (in the analytical sense if you will) their characterological deficiencies. This, I feel, can be much more effectively done within the context of the ongoing program of

SAI. Fritz Redl calls this "participation in the milieu" and "crisis intervention." Whatever you call it, it seems to have relevance to the SAI short-term program.

Financing

Quite simply, a problem existed because it cost so much to conduct the summer program. In 1973, for example, it cost more than $2,200 per student, and more than half a million dollars was spent over the ten-year period through 1973. This clearly influenced the nature of the student population. More specifically, it created the problem of financing the Student Achievement Institute as a whole. No solid way of substantially reducing the cost was discovered, particularly in light of the Institute's policy of using highly qualified professionals.

Recruitment

By the early 1970's SAI was finding it very difficult to recruit students for the summer program. It can be hypothesized that part of the problem was the cost, though less than half was borne by the family of the student and though scholarships were offered. It can also be hypothesized that part of the problem was the significant increase in the number of programs advertising themselves similarly to SAI. Several staff members suggested that the problem was also caused by changing attitudes in the population at large toward the question of underachievement, as well as changes in the relationship between the generations. For example, early in the Institute's history, it seemed that parents decided whether or not their son would come. Later, it appeared that the students themselves made the decision. Given the fact that few students (especially underachievers) relish the idea of spending a summer in a school, this could have had a substantial impact on the student body. Finally, there was a connection with the nation's economy; e.g., one summer when SAI enrollment declined significantly, *camp* enrollment did likewise.

UNRESOLVED ISSUES

What Are Criteria for Success?

What should a program such as the Student Achievement Institute attempt to accomplish? Is the ultimate measure of success improved grades? Is it, instead, the overall psychological development of the student? If so, how is that readily measured? What aspects of psychological development should be considered? These questions not only have a significant influence on the evaluation of results; inevitably, they affect the way the program is conducted. The SAI operated from the assumption that its objective was the broad personal development of the individual student, but it was the clear intent of the founders that this should also lead to improved achievement.

What Were the Results of the Program?

How many students indeed achieved at higher academic levels? For how long? How many remained academic underachievers but truly made gains in other areas? What areas? How measured? To answer these questions, letters of praise and questionnaire data, though provocative, are grossly insufficient.

Are Achievement and Competition "Good"?

Increasingly SAI staff members found themselves facing the kinds of questions being asked in society at large about achievement and competition. Students frequently came armed with the argument that "there's nothing sacred about achievement." Was this to be considered a rationalization and the student's way of avoiding effort, or was this a reflection of a changing social norm? The American socioeconomic system has traditionally been built on the concepts of individual achievement and competition with others. But, as one staff member put it, "Do underachievers have the 'right' to underachieve? Were we not forcefully imposing a value upon adolescents? Our value. While we may have the right to impose, surely the teenager has a right to reject." In a related fashion, are achievement and competition so closely intertwined as to be synonymous? Is it possible to stimulate an individual to compete with himself without also encouraging competition with others, and is that desirable?

One SAI method utilized in every summer program highlights this issue: the awarding of trophies at the concluding banquet. There was not much doubt that it dramatized one of the essential premises of the Student Achievement Institute; namely, that the environment must encourage, recognize, and reward achievement. The process of carrying it out was much more controversial and, in retrospect, it seems remarkable that every year the staff ended up unanimously endorsing the concept. Apparently, the advantages of rewarding special achievements outweighed the disadvantages of "implicit losers" and unclear criteria. (A 1969 staff committee attempt to formulate the problems appears in Appendix D.)

Are the SAI Methods and Model Relevant on a Preventative Basis?

The Institute obviously was dealing with students who were already underachieving. It was also clear that most had been underachieving for a long time. It could be hypothesized that educational environments with SAI-like components might help prevent the problem in the first place. Such an environment applied earlier in the student's life might also cut off the vicious circle of underachievement with greater effectiveness than was possible at SAI. Because of the nature of the Institute and its student population, the specifics of prevention remain unresolved.

Can the Methods and Model Be Translated to a School-Year Program?

The Institute acted as consultant in the development of one nine-month program. While this program incorporated some of the basic techniques of the SAI summer program, the extent to which they were applied as well as the number of students involved were insufficient to provide an answer to this question. In addition, a number of staff members have returned home to their own institutions and adapted techniques developed at the Institute. These instances also fall short of a complete replication of the summer program in a school-year situation.

Is the Model Applicable Only to "Upper-Class" Students?

The financial structure of the Student Achievement Institute tended strongly to preclude boys with limited financial resources. As a result, most of the students came from upper middle-class families. While some were from other socioeconomic groups and while our data suggest no significant differences in the effects of the program, the sample of students from these other backgrounds is so limited that no generalizations can be made. Most students came from families where the head of the household was a professional or in a relatively high-level business position; the values and child-rearing methods to which they were exposed may be significantly different from students raised in different environments.

Can the Model and Methods Be Applied to Female Students?

This clearly is an unresolved issue: The Student Achievement Institute doesn't know. Certainly it can be hypothesized that much of the SAI summer program would be applicable to female students. When the Institute began, in general, boys were more vigorously encouraged to value achievement than girls were. More recently, while a difference probably still exists, it appears to be considerably diminished. If this is the case, then it is quite possible that high school girls would enter into a program such as SAI with attitudes less different from boy students than has been the case in the past. This, in turn, should make the model equally relevant for both sexes.

A related unresolved issue: What would have been the impact of full-time live-in women staff members? Although there were sometimes women on the staff who did not live on campus, and although there were definitely potential difficulties in living logistics (and, therefore, in full role participation), perhaps this would have helped address issues of psychosocial development.

Did the Staff Learn from Experience?

Some staff members felt that the Institute became overly self-conscious in its continual critique of itself. Other staff members felt that the Institute was sometimes guilty of learning the same thing five different times, rather than learning five new things. The staff did find it exceptionally difficult to commit itself actively to systematic research in addition to all the day-to-day activities. Efforts to bring in outside research personnel met with mixed results. An unresolved issue, then, has to do with the whole process of conducting and evaluating research into the problem of underachievement, while simultaneously providing direct services.

Did SAI Accomplish Its Objectives?

It appears that SAI did meet the first two of the objectives which were listed in its bylaws: (1) A summer program for underachieving students was conducted over ten years with 254 students drawn from thirty states and three foreign countries, and (2) the available data suggest that they were helped to achieve higher levels of personal effectiveness—at very least, the students, parents, and staff who participated appear to be convinced.

As for the objectives of training academic and psychological personnel in dealing with underachieving students and their problems, participating staff members definitely felt they were "trained." Attempts were made to train other people as well, including a number of graduate students who served as part-time staff members, and the non-SAI teachers who worked with SAI students in their classes. However, the number of individuals involved in all training efforts is small: not over a hundred. This report is in part an attempt to extend our observations to other professionals.

It is perhaps an unresolved issue whether (a) research was done in identifying the causes of underachieving and (b) diagnostic and developmental methods and tools were developed. Most of the people involved agree that the Institute did not succeed in conducting the kind and quality of research that had been hoped for. Diagnostic and developmental methods and tools, however, were certainly developed and applied.

Given the nature of the "research" conducted by the Institute, this report fulfills the fifth of its objectives. It publishes the results of one experiment in dealing with underachievement.

Is Underachievement a Viable Concept?

This final issue has begun to emerge in the professional literature and, by implication, in recent legislation concerning young people with "special needs." As Dr. Kornrich has suggested in his article "What Ever Happened to Underachievement?" (reprinted in Appendix G, primarily for interested professionals), the question of "underachievement" versus "learning disability" versus "minimal brain dysfunction" is more than a semantic issue. It is an issue which seems to imply not only different causes but also different ways of attempting to help. It seems to have successfully confused lay people and professionals alike.

Parents, students, and some staff members came to SAI feeling that confusion. Some left feeling it, too, and predictably SAI did not provide "a final answer." Labels often seemed to provide convenient rationalizations and excuses rather than constructive impetus. While the program explicitly *did not* attempt to serve students with demonstrable neurological damage, it *did* attempt to provide an environment in which students could do something about behavior over which they had control. The Student Achievement Institute seemed to demonstrate that some "underachievement" could be affected; that it was possible to

provide students a chance for change.

Appendixes

Appendix A

Board of Directors
1964-1978

Frank L. Boyden
Headmaster
Deerfield Academy

Robert E. Butler, Ph.D.
Headmaster
Tilton School

Joseph H. Chadbourne, Jr.
Headmaster
Tilton School

John A. Clizbe, Ph.D.
Partner
Nordli, Wilson Associates

Milton Cohen
Vice President and General Manager
Hertz Systems, Inc.

Note: The members are identified by the position held during their tenure on the Board.

98

George I. Davis
Chairman of the Board
Glens Falls Insurance Company

John B. Davis, Jr., Ph.D.
Superintendent of Schools
Minneapolis, Minnesota

Richard Ward Day, Ph.D.
Principal
The Phillips Exeter Academy

Burte Guterman, M.D.
Psychiatrist

Neil W. Halkyard
Headmaster
Shepherd Knapp School

Francis A. Harrington
Vice President
The Paul Revere Life Insurance Company

Frank L. Harrington
Chairman of the Board
The Paul Revere Life Insurance Company

Hudson Hoagland, Ph.D.
President
Worcester Foundation for Experimental Biology

William D. Ireland, Jr.
President
Guaranty Bank and Trust Company

Frederick H. Jackson, Ph.D.
President
Clark University

John Jeppson
Chairman of the Board
Norton Company

Milton Kornrich, Ph.D.
Psychologist

William C. Kvaraceus, Ph.D.
Chairman, Department of Education
Clark University

Laurence H. Lougee
Partner
Mirick, O'Connell, DeMallie and Lougee

Herbert B. Moore
Headmaster
Tilton School

William Nordli, Ph.D.
Partner
Nordli, Wilson Associates

William S. Piper, Jr., Ed.D.
Headmaster
Worcester Academy

David M. Pynchon
Headmaster
Deerfield Academy

Frances L. Reid
Administrative Assistant
Nordli, Wilson Associates

Daniel Catton Rich
Director
Worcester Art Museum

Appleton H. Seaverns
Headmaster
Suffield Academy

Robert E. Smith, Ph.D.
Executive Director, General Programs
Educational Testing Service

J. Watson Wilson, Ph.D.
Managing Partner
Nordli, Wilson Associates

Appendix B

Schedule of a Typical Week

1969 STUDENT ACHIEVEMENT INSTITUTE

NAME: MARTIN

	MONDAY	TUESDAY	WEDNESDAY	THURSDAY	FRIDAY	SATURDAY AND SUNDAY	SPECIAL ACTIVITIES
8:00 A.M.	CLASS	CLASS	CLASS	CLASS	CLASS		
9:00 A.M.	STUDY HALL	STUDY HALL	STUDY HALL	STUDY HALL	STUDY HALL		
10:00 A.M.	Project group	Individual psychotherapy		Project group	Individual psychotherapy		
11:00 A.M.			Academic (staff) counselor				
Noon	LUNCH	LUNCH	LUNCH	LUNCH	LUNCH		
1:00 P.M.	Session with academic (staff) counselor	Group psychotherapy		Group psychotherapy			
2:00 P.M.			Developmental reading		Developmental reading		

	Psychology of Achievement in Life—LECTURE	Psychology of Achievement in Life—SEMINAR	LECTURE	SEMINAR	Dormitory conference and student government	
3:00 P.M.						NOTE: Unscheduled time will, in most instances, be used for special conferences, independent projects, and self-initiated activities.
4:00 P.M.	Athletics and/or physical fitness	Athletics, etc., intergroup competition	Athletics, etc.	Athletics, etc.	Athletics, etc.	
6:00 P.M.	DINNER	DINNER	DINNER	DINNER	DINNER	
7:15 P.M.	Instructional movie and *discussion*	Electives and special interest groups	Speaker and discussion	Electives and special interest groups	Entertainment and social	
9:00 P.M.	Special study group	Special study group	Special study group	Special study group		Sunday evening study hall
10:45 P.M.	Achievement oriented sleep					

Appendix C

Sample
Psychological Report

This report contains the results of a psychological study that has been made to determine the nature and extent of the personal characteristics, interests, and aptitudes of the individual under consideration.

> Report on: Larry
> Age: 16
> School: Student Achievement
> Institute

Intellectual Characteristics

Intellectually, Larry is functioning in the very superior range of intelligence. His capacity in certain social science areas appears even higher. However, he has rarely fully utilized his amazing intellectual ability because of various emotional reasons. When the *going gets tough,* he finds himself unprepared with skills and drive to measure up to high level learning and achievement expectations.

Larry tends to use his intelligence more in "thinking" and

talking than in "doing." As a result, he's found himself "frustrated, because I know I can do it." He is generally falling below his expected achievement in most major subject matter areas.

Larry exhibits exceptional comprehension and abstract reasoning power. He is very analytic in his thinking process, but has poor habits to accompany this strength. Basically, Larry applies his intellect to "doing" in spurts, rather than in long, persistent thrusts.

He has no major difficulty in making decisions or in readiness to give opinions. Sometimes his judgments are not as sound as they could be, because he sometimes gets angry when he is right and is not properly heard. More often, however, he withdraws from forcing a point that he believes is correct.

Emotional Characteristics

Emotionally, Larry shows fairly good stability from an overall point of view. However, he indicates short-lived interests in things and tends to be indifferent to his surroundings at times. He's usually fairly easily turned off, when things aren't "relevant or meaningful." However, at the Institute he attempted sincerely to make things relevant. Unfortunately, relevancy in some areas existed only in spurts. For Larry, it's as if he jumps in fast and hard and tries to get everything he can from a situation and then becomes turned off.

As a result of this "in-and-out" pattern, Larry often finds himself more disinterested and frustrated than he would like to feel. If he were a leader, he would find himself less frustrated, but as a regular group member, he gets impatient quickly. One of the reasons for this emotional characteristic is that Larry is being driven by two conflicting forces. On the one hand, he would like to be a friendly, considerate, popular, well-liked person—one of the guys. But on the other hand, he has tendencies to be powerful and forceful and dominant. Unfortunately, he feels that these latter qualities would come out in negativistic ways, should he give vent to this aspect of his personality.

The feeling that he would come across negatively is directly related to his great concern about trust. He subtly questions the sincerity of others, whether they are interested in him for his own sake. But, on occasion, he takes the blame onto himself and feels very unhappy and angry toward himself.

He is somewhat careful to avoid being thought of negatively by others. For example, he generally wants the other person to commit himself to the conversation or relationship first. In his words, he is "dependent on others to break the ice with me; I need a catalyst to set off a relationship or conversation." In this regard, he considers himself to be "not the most outwardly open person with people, sometimes shy or cautious; sometimes more of a follower than a leader, especially in unknown situations." In this and other respects, he opts for a low-risk approach to problem solving.

Maturationally, Larry is fairly well developed. He is not a very anxious or worried person. He holds his own and often demonstrates exceptional leadership qualities among peers. He is a marvelously comfortable guy, probably one of his strongest personality characteristics. He has a pleasant friendliness and a warm, sincere smile. Sometimes, however, he gets somewhat angry at himself, or others, and tends to come across pessimistically, turning his anger inward at himself.

Larry adjusts fairly well and rapidly. Although he does approach new situations cautiously, he rapidly becomes involved and comfortable.

Probably Larry's most difficult adjustment at this time is in academics. The core of the emotional factors which is related to his adjustment struggles is a "measuring up" need. Larry, to a large extent unconsciously, feels that he must meet exceptionally high standards from others. He has not developed the necessary ingredient of achievement for his own sake. This pattern of "achievement for others" has helped Larry raise his tolerance for the pain of disappointing schoolwork. He experiences a considerable amount of guilt when he feels that he is not "measuring up." Hence, he loses in whatever direction he chooses: A's for others; or C's and D's without trying, but with the resultant guilt. Until he can *do it for himself,* and maybe with some help from others, he'll be "spinning his wheels." What others who are important to Larry have not fully realized, at least on an emotional level, is that *he can only achieve if it is for himself!*

Motivational Characteristics

Motivationally, Larry is a very independent and unyielding individual, somebody reluctant to compromise and sometimes convinced he is absolutely right. Going along with this is a concern of his being used by others at times. He tends to be a fairly short-term operator in terms of goal planning and is unable to sustain really long-term efforts. In general, he is a fairly casual individual, somebody who dislikes restrictions and is flexible and unprepared in many situations. He dislikes systematic approaches. Remarkably, though, he also exhibits a subtle and conflicting need for emotional support from others.

Larry is more motivated in fun situations, like sports and messing around. He is an active and highly motivated outdoorsman. However, in systematic situations, he tends to tune out to a degree. He describes himself as becoming "lazy, daydreaming too much, uncommitted, and generally trying to absorb things passively."

He seems unsure of his ability to obtain social rewards and so has considered these unimportant. On the other hand, he would like to be more persuasive and stronger than he currently perceives himself to be.

Academically, Larry seems to experience a decrease in motivation when pushed by others to do the work. This extra pressure is experienced as "achieving for someone else," and it falls right into the "measuring-up" syndrome described above.

Insight Characteristics

Larry has developed fairly good insight into himself. His efforts have immeasurably increased this insight during the Institute. What he has most difficulty understanding about himself is his on-and-off performance and his "laziness." He knows and describes these personal characteristics but he gets frustrated when he can't see a tangible reason for their existence. In this regard, Larry is only now beginning to have some appreciation for unconscious motivation, and in light of his "measuring-up" feelings, he has developed a greater understanding of some of the *why*'s of his behavior and feelings. His insights about himself have mostly been, heretofore, of a descriptive sort. He has been learning how to be introspective in ways that facilitate his better understanding of his feelings.

Larry's insights into the behavior of others are also fairly well developed now. For example, he is very capable of giving accurate feedback about peers and adults. Unfortunately, he is bothered at times by his perceptivity, because he feels that he'll come across a little too strong.

Skill in Human Relations

Socially, Larry is a likable, congenial person, somebody who is seen as honest. He would like to be more fair and frank but he holds back in some areas. Being genuine is very important to him, and he would work well if he perceived that some authority were genuinely interested in helping him.

Larry makes friends easily and has a great strength in his ease of meeting and talking with people, both peers and adults. He is mostly pleasant and fun to be with and sophisticated in social graces. He has an appealing easygoing manner and always tries to get along well with others.

His overall personality style is very well integrated socially, although he has not begun to seriously consider girls at this time. This should come with increased confidence and experimentation.

His social skills probably hold a clue as to the sort of adult he can become. For one thing, he likes people and he wants to be with people, although at times when he's feeling guilty about his level of academic achievement, he'd rather be away from certain people. His talent for putting others at ease and his very superior warmth can enable him to fit nicely into various people-oriented vocational and occupational areas.

Academic and Vocational Implications

He has earned lower marks than has been *expected*. The work *he has done,* considering the personal pressure, in some respects, could be considered nothing less than phenomenal. He has always been in the shadow of extraordinary achievement in every direction he turns. He has been coerced, bribed, and challenged to "achieve high." It has never really been communicated to Larry that he needs to do nothing more than to develop and meet his *own* standards. As a result of all of this pressure, Larry has been unable to escape from the "measuring-up" phenomenon which engulfs his life.

Larry hasn't wanted to, but he has, nonetheless, found himself much more interested in having fun than doing work. Affluent recreational opportunities have been encouraged, which is certainly healthy in itself. Unfortunately, Larry has turned more to these "fun opportunities" to develop positive self-feelings, because he has been unable to get the *positive* support he needed in academic and emotional areas. Too much energy goes into having fun, but this is understandable in light of the impossible pressure he faces in all other areas.

Through the years, Larry has gotten by on the strength of his intelligence alone, and has not learned how to concentrate and properly approach academics, test situations, and all other dimensions of the learning process. He finds himself, now, very tense about studying, because he has only fair habits and must constantly deal with the question, "Do I really want to do it?"

Vocationally, the Strong indicates interest in physical types of occupations, like osteopath, physician, and physical therapist. As well, he has significant interests in the social service and social science areas. He seems to be heading in the direction of the latter areas.

Summary and Recommendations

Larry is a bright, sensitive, well-liked person, who is often harder on himself than he needs to be. He wants to be liked and respected for "who he is," not what others want "him to become." In one sense, he has been on the *defensive* all of his life, trying desperately to "measure up" to the impossible standards set by others. What he's really trying to tell everyone concerned with him is that he wants to "be his own man," to be regarded as Larry—a unique and worthwhile *individual*.

Until he escapes entirely from the measuring-up pressures or until he is taken to be the warm and genuine person he really is, it is unlikely that his terrible frustrated feelings can be channeled into productive, *self-satisfying* achievement.

At the Institute, Larry has done more than he's ever before accomplished in recognizing that he is a worthwhile and acceptable individual. He has felt the positive feelings of being genuinely accepted by his peers and staff, and he has gained considerable regard for his talents and strengths. He has been a self-developed leader in many areas of the program, and he has served exceptionally well in this capacity. He is still not willing to fully recognize that *others want* him to "take charge" more and assert his dominance and persuasive power, but he is coming to terms with these issues. He has done well in his academic course and has worked seriously on his concentration powers and skills. This course, mathematics, was probably the most difficult course he could have taken.

As Larry returns home, the biggest problem he will be facing is fear, associated with the potential guilt he will feel if he senses the *other-imposed pressures* and cannot make the mark. On the other hand, because of the fondness and regard for significant others in his family and elsewhere, he will be sensitive to any different kind of support he may receive. We hope that whatever changes you may notice in Larry are accepted by you. We have not encouraged anti-parental behavior or attitudes in the students, but we have encouraged a development of self-identity and independent growth. As an outgrowth of this self-identity, Larry may challenge some issues, values, or opinions that he has not challenged before. We would like you to appreciate these challenges and accept them as a function of healthy growth and normal maturation.

To support the work that we and Larry have done during the past six weeks, we recommend that you consider the following possibilities:

1. After Larry has been home for a period of time, the family (Larry, Mom, and Dad) would be advised to review this report independently and together.

2. A very major attitudinal decision must be made and implemented by Larry's parents. That is whether or not to continue creating "measuring-up" situations academically and otherwise. Remarks such as, "Why are you procrastinating?" are perceived as "measuring up." If the decision is to communicate in ways that will help develop and continue to support Larry's development of his *own set* of values and standards, then much can be accomplished. For example, Larry should *never* be allowed to feel guilt unless it is provoked by his own inadequate performance on his own goal system. On the other hand, Larry should continue to develop and learn how to communicate to his parents and others "what" *his system* is becoming. Granted, this may take several years, but every effort in this direction will be time well spent.

3. Larry should continue to develop and be helped to develop all of his strengths, i.e., his warm and positive personality, his aggressiveness, his skill in relating with people, his insights into self and others, his abstract thinking and reading.

4. Larry should develop a new and different relationship with his father. He desperately wants and needs this *now*. For example, if the two of them could go into the city for dinner occasionally, or to a soccer game, or sailing or hiking or skiing together, every moment spent together would be beneficial in getting to know each other better.

Although Larry will be going away to college soon, the relationship he has with his father is just as vitally important then. Their communication (letters, phone calls, visits home, summers) doesn't need to center on what grades he's making, but rather on what experiences he is having. Larry can handle his own academics better, if left alone by his parents. This may have to come as a long hard struggle, and he may not *measure up* to what everyone has told him all his life, but he'll certainly be able to develop and maintain a very worthwhile set of self-satisfying values—of which both he and his parents (if they want to) can be justly proud.

Father's involvement with Larry *must* be real and consistent. Sometimes *other things should be secondary* to this relationship.

5.   Larry is under a lot of personal pressure as he is attempting to become his "own man." For example, he (unfortunately) feels at times that "I should change for them, rather than they for me; I should try to spend more time with my father, rather than vice versa; I should stop being selfish in that respect." The fact of this matter is that he is expressing irrational guilt, guilt he neither needs to or should feel. It would be vital that he learn how to do away with this guilt, and that his father take the initiative more.

6.   Participation in team sports, i.e. soccer, will be vitally important as an opportunity for him to continue to test out many of the relevant insights he has developed. Sports also will provide an important avenue for continued physical development and emotional development.

7.   The entire matter of college planning needs to be considered by the family, in light of his development during the Institute. It is recommended that this matter be discussed, briefly, at the final interview, and that Mr. _____ share his insights here.

Larry has made some strides in his personal and academic development during these past six weeks. Both of us will be available at any time during the coming year to handle any questions or recommendations which may arise.

(Signed) _____   (Signed) _____
Psychologist   Academic Counselor
(address)   (address)

Appendix D

Comments
on SAI Awards

At this point in the Institute, an elaborate evaluation of the award program simply isn't possible. In fact, it may not even be possible to achieve a complete or final consensus concerning either the value or the meaning of specific or all awards. Nevertheless, we should each confront our own feelings concerning the following kinds of issues:

1. What are we attempting to accomplish with the awards?
2. Are we recognizing or rewarding certain kinds of behavior, or are we also attempting to consider broader psychological issues (for example, would it help or hurt the boy to receive an award)?
3. Do we wish to utilize primarily objective measures or are we equally accepting of the staff's "gut-level" considerations?
4. For "spirit" kinds of awards, are we talking about behavior during the entire Institute or during later segments of the Institute?
5. For "improvement" awards, are we speaking of improvement relative to performance prior to the Institute or relative to performance at the initial stages of the Institute?

Note: This study was made by a staff committee during the summer of 1969.

115

6. How concerned are we with a distribution of awards across teams?

7. How concerned are we with the issue of more than one award to a single individual?

These questions are by no means all-inclusive, and probably they will only help each of us to confront other questions which we each hold. Below are listed some ways of viewing each of the awards.

SPIRIT OF SAI

1. The individual who seems to have "caught hold" of the intent of the Institute.

2. One who seeks self-improvement as exemplified by actions and deeds.

3. One who has shown improvement, however general.

4. One who has demonstrated a genuine concern for constructive change: behavioral, attitudinal, insightful.

5. Someone who has gradually or abruptly changed during the Institute; or someone who came here obviously determined to undergo immediate change.

DIRECTOR'S AWARDS (2)

1. Quite frankly, second and third place in the "spirit" contest.

2. Someone who changed just as much as the "spirit" winner, but whose change occurred later.

3. Someone whose change was less all-encompassing or dramatic.

4. Someone who demonstrated the ability to assist others in changing, though perhaps exhibited somewhat less constructive change in himself.

BEST STUDENT

1. Highest scholastic average at the Institute, or
2. A high average in combination with outstanding study habits, or
3. Best study habits.

MOST IMPROVED STUDENT

1. One who shows the greatest improvement in academic performance from the beginning to the end of the six-week period.
2. One who shows the greatest improvement in academic tasks relative to his performance prior to attending the Institute.

BEST ATHLETE

1. Student who is the best all-around athlete, both in ability and character.
2. Student who is the best all-around athlete in ability and utilization of that ability.
3. Student who competes most effectively as a team member.

MOST IMPROVED ATHLETE

1. One who shows the greatest improvement in general ability.
2. Student who shows greatest improvement in competitive attitudes and cooperativeness.
3. Student who, compared with his approach at the beginning of the Institute, demonstrated the greatest ability to compensate for initial physical or attitudinal shortcomings. In other words, the one who tried hard even though he had nothing to try with.

SPECIAL SAI AWARD

1. The student who deserved to get something.
2. The student who has realized a special or relatively isolated achievement.
3. The student who has been an outstanding leader.
4. The student voted by his peers as most indicative of something-or-other.
5. The someone who has done something in some way.
6. The student who made some kind of unique contribution.
7. The student who would benefit from receiving some kind of award.

Obviously, we have a complex task before us. Fortunately, a poll of the staff did indicate a unanimity in at least one area— the rewards must reflect the best interests of the students and their accomplishments rather than those of the staff. That alone is no easy "achievement."

Appendix E

Sample Research Questionnaires

SAI STAFF QUESTIONNAIRE—OCTOBER 1973

Please tell us about your SAI experience, especially in terms of its meaningfulness for *you*. Feel free to give us as much additional information as you like.

I. At this point, how do you rate your SAI experience for *you*?

      Very   Valuable   Of Some   Of Little   Not
    Valuable   Value   Value   Valuable

II. To what degree do you feel your SAI experience has contributed, is contributing, or will contribute to you in the following areas? (Circle 1 for very positive, 2 for quite positive, 3 for so-so, 4 for very little contribution, or 5 for didn't or won't really help at all.)

    A. overall professional competence (ability to do your job better, etc.)

1	2	3	4	5
very positive		so-so		not at all

119

B. effectiveness with adolescents (ability to help, etc.)

        1   2   3   4   5

very positive   so-so   not at all

C. specific useable techniques (new skills to apply, etc.)

        1   2   3   4   5

very positive   so-so   not at all

D. ideas for implementation (systems changes, guidance for colleagues, etc.)

        1   2   3   4   5

very positive   so-so   not at all

E. insight into individual adolescents (awareness of needs, understanding of feelings, etc.)

        1   2   3   4   5

very positive   so-so   not at all

F. understanding of underachievement (insight into causes, etc.)

        1   2   3   4   5

very positive   so-so   not at all

G. your own *personal* growth (self-confidence, maturity, etc.)

        1   2   3   4   5

very positive   so-so   not at all

H. research endeavors (studies conducted, publications, etc.)

        1   2   3   4   5

very positive   so-so   not at all

III. What one word best describes the Student Achievement Institute from your point of view? Write the first word that occurs to you.

_____

IV. From your point of view, in what ways did SAI contribute most to you (what you "got out of it," most rewarding aspects, etc.)?

_____
_____
_____
_____

V. From your point of view, in what ways was SAI *not* as helpful to you as you would have liked (didn't meet your hopes and expectations, etc.)?

_____
_____
_____
_____

VI. In what specific ways, if any, have you applied or do you expect to apply your SAI experience?

_____
_____
_____
_____

VII. Additional comments:

_____
_____
_____
_____

Year(s) associated with SAI (optional)_____

SAI ALUMNI QUESTIONNAIRE—OCTOBER 1973

Please tell us about your SAI experience by checking or filling in the items below. Feel free to give us any additional information you would like. We recognize that some questions may be more applicable than others, but your thoroughness will be helpful.

I.   At this time, how do you rate your SAI experience? (Circle one)

     Very   Valuable   Of Some   Of Little   Not
     Valuable   Value   Value   Valuable

II. To what degree do you feel your SAI experience has contributed, is contributing, or will contribute to you in the following areas? (Circle 1 for very positive contribution, 2 for quite positive, 3 for so-so, 4 for very little contribution, or 5 for didn't or won't help at all.)

A. academic effectiveness (grades, study skills, attitude toward school, etc.)

     1   2   3   4   5

---

     very positive   so-so   not at all

B. extracurricular effectiveness (clubs and organizations, athletics, avocations, etc.)

     1   2   3   4   5

---

     very positive   so-so   not at all

C. vocational effectiveness (full or part-time job success and satisfaction. etc.)

     1   2   3   4   5

---

     very positive   so-so   not at all

D. relationships with parents (ability to get along, mutual understanding, communications, etc.)

    1   2   3   4   5

    ---

    very positive   so-so   not at all

E. relationships with peers (social skills, friendships, leadership, followership, etc.)

    1   2   3   4   5

    ---

    very positive   so-so   not at all

F. relationships with teachers and bosses (ability to work together, communications, etc.)

    1   2   3   4   5

    ---

    very positive   so-so   not at all

G. your own emotional adjustment (self-confidence, self-acceptance, maturity, ability to cope, etc.)

    1   2   3   4   5

    ---

    very positive   so-so   not at all

H. your own motivation (drive, stamina, desire to achieve, etc.)

    1   2   3   4   5

    ---

    very positive   so-so   not at all

I. your self-awareness (understanding of strengths and shortcomings, etc.)

    1   2   3   4   5

    ---

    very positive   so-so   not at all

III. What one word best describes the Student Achievement Institute from your point of view? Write the first word that occurs to you.

_____

IV. From your point of view, in what ways did SAI contribute most to you (satisfactions, constructive changes, later benefits, etc.)?

_____
_____
_____
_____

V. From your point of view, in what ways was SAI *not* as helpful to you as you would have liked (aims not accomplished, weaknesses unchanged, etc.)?

_____
_____
_____
_____

VI. Tell us about your academic experiences since leaving SAI (schools attended, diplomas or degrees, grades, special recognition, etc.).

_____
_____
_____
_____

VII. Tell us about your "extracurricular" experiences since leaving SAI (group participation, leadership experiences, recognitions, etc.).

_____
_____
_____

VIII. Tell us about your vocational experiences since leaving SAI (jobs held full or part-time, etc.).

_____
_____
_____
_____

IX. Additional comments:

_____
_____
_____
_____

Name (optional)_____

SAI PARENTS' QUESTIONNAIRE—OCTOBER 1973

Please tell us about your son's SAI experience by checking or filling in the items below. Feel free to give us any additional information you would like. We recognize that some questions may be more applicable than others, but your thoroughness will be helpful.

I. At this time, how do you rate your son's SAI experience? (Circle one)

Very   Valuable Of Some   Of Little   Not
Valuable   Value   Value   Valuable

II. To what degree do you feel your son's SAI experience has contributed, is contributing, or will contribute to him in the following areas? (Circle 1 for very positive, 2 for quite positive, 3 for so-so, 4 for very little contribution, or 5 for didn't or won't really help at all.)

A. academic effectiveness (grades, study skills, attitude toward school, etc.)

1	2	3	4	5

very positive   so-so   not at all

B. extracurricular effectiveness (clubs and organizations, athletics, avocations, etc.)

   1   2   3   4   5

   ---

   very positive   so-so   not at all

C. vocational effectiveness (full or part-time job success and satisfaction, etc.)

   1   2   3   4   5

   ---

   very positive   so-so   not at all

D. relationships with parents (ability to get along, mutual understanding, communications, etc.)

   1   2   3   4   5

   ---

   very positive   so-so   not at all

E. relationships with peers (social skills, friendships, leadership, followership, etc.)

   1   2   3   4   5

   ---

   very positive   so-so   not at all

F. relationships with teachers and bosses (ability to work together, communications, etc.)

   1   2   3   4   5

   ---

   very positive   so-so   not at all

G. his emotional adjustment (self-confidence, self-acceptance, maturity, ability to cope, etc.)

   1   2   3   4   5

   ---

   very positive   so-so   not at all

H. his motivation (drive, stamina, desire to achieve, etc.)

1	2	3	4	5

very positive	so-so	not at all

I. his self-awareness (understanding of strengths and shortcomings, etc.)

1	2	3	4	5

very positive	so-so	not at all

III. What one word best describes the Student Achievement Institute from your point of view? Write the first word that occurs to you.

_____

IV. From your point of view, in what ways did SAI contribute most to *your son* (what he "got out of it," constructive changes, later benefits, etc.)?

_____
_____
_____
_____

V. From your point of view, in what ways was SAI *not* as helpful to *your son* as you would have liked (aims not accomplished, weaknesses unchanged, etc.)?

_____
_____
_____
_____

VI.   From your point of view, in what ways (if any) was SAI helpful to you personally?

_____

_____

_____

_____

VII. From your point of view, in what ways did SAI prove *not* to be as helpful to you as you would have liked?

_____

_____

_____

_____

VIII. Additional comments:

_____

_____

_____

_____

Name (optional)_____

Appendix F

Brief Annotated Underachievement Bibliography

A. FOR STUDENTS

1. *Elementary*

Berger, T. *I Have Feelings.* New York: Human Sciences Press, 1971.

Although a great deal has been written about you, actually you are the forgotten child when it comes to anything written *for you* concerning difficulties with school work (the fancy word for this difficulty is called "underachievement"). We promise that we will write something for you shortly, so that maybe you can have some understanding as to why school or certain subjects are so difficult for you, and why so often your teachers and parents or guardians may seem angry with you because of your difficulties. It's really not your fault, you know. One small, beautiful book that you can certainly read by yourself, that can give you some idea about all the different kinds of feelings you have (your feelings can affect your school work), is the book by Terry Berger.

2. *Secondary and College*

Bricklin, B., and P. M. Bricklin. *Bright Child Poor Grades: The Psychology of Underachievement*. New York: Delacorte Press, 1967.

This book is a good introduction and overview of the significant problem of academic underachievement. While you may have a very simple explanation for academic difficulties (e.g., you were told you were "lazy"), we can assure you that underachievement is a much more complex matter. The authors relate underachievement to such factors as the fear of success, inner doubts, the overprotective mother, the boy who is afraid to be a sissy, aggression, competition, etc.

Halpern, H. M. Can psychotherapy help the underachiever? In H. M. Halpern, *A Parent's Guide to Child Psychotherapy*. New York: A. S. Barnes, 1963.

This gem of an article written for parents and professionals, but certainly understandable by you, gives a brilliant explanation of the psychological factors (often unconscious) involved in academic underachievement. ". . . In the underachiever something goes wrong. Instead of trying to see himself as a separate individual through accomplishing, he does it by not accomplishing."

Harris, I. D. *Emotional Blocks to Learning*. New York: Free Press of Glencoe, 1961.

An easily readable, research-oriented book describing the many factors (e.g., social class, family disorganization, parental ambition, birth order, aggression, submission, etc.) that singly or interactively have an impact on achievement. "In order to learn, one must have enough free aggressive energy to be inquisitive, to penetrate, and to persevere against obstacles. One must feel enough angry frustration in order to cope strenuously with an unsatisfying situation."

Sarnoff, I., and T. Raphael. Five failing college students. *American Journal of Orthopsychiatry*, 1955, *25*, 343-77.

Too often articles about underachievement in college

students are either too superficial, theoretical, or both. However, in this exceptional paper, Drs. Sarnoff and Raphael deeply and thoroughly enter the lives of five male college freshmen, with the result that the reader emerges with a rather solid understanding of the factors contributing to each student's difficulties with academic work. "Despite the small size of our sample, a surprisingly wide gamut of failure-inducing factors was brought to view—physical, mental, social, economic, intrinsic and extrinsic, underlying and immediate, and in various constellations."

B. FOR PARENTS

Bricklin and Bricklin
   See above.
Doll, R. C., and R. S. Fleming, eds. *Children Under Pressure.* Columbus, Ohio: Charles E. Merrill, 1966.
   In this book, one of the pressures discussed is the pressure to achieve academically. "Education is a serious business; it ought not, however, to be a grim and desperate one. It ought to be possible to learn without tears—and surely without nervous breakdowns." There are other quotes and ideas worthy of your perusal.
Gardner, R. A. A girl with psychogenic learning disorders (chapter 14). In R. A. Gardner, *Therapeutic Communication with Children: Mutual Storytelling Technique in Child Psychotherapy.* New York: Science House, 1971.
   In typically brilliant Richard Gardner style, the effect of parental attitudes (e.g., the overprotective parent, "rich man's son syndrome," etc.) upon academic achievement are reviewed. Also, in the presentation of a nine-year-old girl with learning difficulties (see, not only boys underachieve) we see the possible relationship between emotional conflict and academic difficulties. It's not easy reading, and though written for the professional, it's too valuable to be missed by parents, professional or otherwise.
Ginott, H. G. *Teacher and Child.* New York: Macmillan Co., 1972.

Read especially the chapters: "Homework" (e.g., "Life is easier when parents deliberately ignore the daily details of their child's homework") and "Tales of Motivations" (e.g., a sign in a classroom: "1. In this class it is permissible to make mistakes; 2. An error is not a terror; 3. Goofs are lessons; 4. You may err, but don't excuse it; 5. Mistakes are for correcting; 6. Value your correction, not your error; 7. Don't let failure go to your head."). Dr. Ginott's previous books, *Between Parent and Child* and *Between Parent and Teenager* also merit your attention, for they skillfully deal with typical parent-child, parent-teenager "hassles."

Halpern

See above. (Read the entire paper, especially "What can the parent do?" and "Counseling for the underachiever's parents.")

Halpern, H. M. Therapy with anti-achievers. *Voices,* 1966, *2,* 95-100.

Anything written by Dr. Halpern is right to the point—the point being the psychological factors, primarily unconscious, related to underachievement. In this paper the parent can more specifically see his approach toward therapy with the underachiever.

Harris

See above.

Iscoe, I. "I told you so": The logical dilemma of the bright underachieving child. *Psychology in the Schools,* 1964, *1,* 282-84.

This particular paper deals with only one but quite important facet of underachievement—namely, the underachiever's highly sensitive reaction to "I told you so"—when he begins to achieve. "If he succeeds further, instead of getting credit, he will only be shown up as not having tried previously."

Kornrich, M. It's not good enough. *Psychology in the Schools,* January, 1966.

This brief paper was stimulated by Iscoe's paper. It describes an unfortunate parental reaction in which the child is told,

even after his grades improved, "It's still not good enough."
As a parent, we ask you to *feel* what this must be like to
hear.
Sarnoff and Raphael
    See above.

C. FOR PROFESSIONALS

Barsch, R. H. Perspectives in learning disabilities: the vectors of
    a new convergence. *Journal of Learning Disabilities,* 1968, *1,*
    7-23.
    Barsch reminds us of what we all know and sometimes
    forget; namely, that difficulties in learning are not the
    province of any one discipline nor does any single explana-
    tion excel in explanatory power over any other explanation
    at this point in time. (Although written in 1968, we take
    the liberty of stating that it is unlikely that Barsch has
    altered his viewpoint. If he has, we have not.)
Camp, B. W. Current thoughts about learning disabilities.
    Journal American Medical Woman's Association, 1976, *31,*
    433-40.
    Although at SAI we assumed a rather "intuitive" definition
    of underachievement, the question of definition is rather
    complex. This fine paper, modestly entitled, reviews some
    of the issues (theoretical and practical) of defining a learn-
    ing problem in reading. While too new to be mentioned in
    Dr. Camp's paper, the federal definition of learning dis-
    ability involves the use of a formula.
Coleman, J. S. The adolescent subculture and academic achieve-
    ment. *American Journal of Sociology,* 1960, *65,* 337-47.
    In our increasing stress upon organic factors and learning
    and our continuing stress upon psychological and social
    class factors, we often overlook the variable of the adoles-
    cent subculture and the "pull" of its value system. Dr. Cole-
    man asked teenagers in ten different high schools, among
    other questions, "How would you like to be remembered
    in school: as an athletic star, a brilliant student, or most

popular?" Surely you can guess the results. Would this be
true seventeen years later, in 1977?

Davidson, H. H., and J. W. Greenberg. *School Achievers from a
Deprived Background.* New York: Associated Educational
Services Corporation, 1967.

This superb study requiring a book to describe, based upon
cautious research, unfortunately did not receive the reader-
ship and attention it merits. The authors, responding to the
fact that most underachievement research is definitely lopsided in the direction of the bright achiever, address themselves to a group of low- and high-achieving lower-class
black youngsters. They were primarily interested, again most
rare in underachievement research, in those factors contributing to success in achievement.

Gardner
See above.

Harris
See above.

Halpern
See above. For additional papers by Halpern see: *Psychoanalytic Review,* 1964, *51,* 173-89; *Psychoanalytic Review,*
1966, *53,* 407-17.

Kornrich, M., ed. *Underachievement.* Springfield, Illinois:
Charles C. Thomas, 1965.

Fifty-one papers describe psychodynamic and socio-cultural
factors contributing to underachievement at elementary,
secondary, and college levels as well as a variety of treatment methods—group and individual counseling, perceptual
training, modified educational environment, home visitation,
etc. Were this book to be revised, it would certainly include
many more treatment methods, e.g., rational-emotive and
other cognitive therapies, marathon and sensitivity groups,
meditation, family therapy, and behavior modification.

Newman, C. J., Dember, C. F., and Krug, O. He can but he
won't—a psychodynamic study of so-called gifted underachievers. *Psychoanalytic Study of the Child,* 1973, *28,* 83-129.

The theoretical concepts of Piaget and psychoanalysis are

brilliantly used and fused in a study of fifteen boys, ages 7-13. The paper reviews their characteristics, e.g., verbalizations, nonverbal behavior, parental attitudes, and difficulties. According to the authors, the developmental story would unfold thusly:

I can, but I won't
I won't, so I don't
I don't, so I can't
I can't, but I'll say I won't.

Raph, J. B., M. L. Goldberg, and A. H. Passow. *Bright Under-achievers.* New York: Teachers College Press, 1966.

This skillfully written and organized book includes one of the finest reviews of underachievement research available (e.g., personality, adjustment, personality traits, self-ratings, home backgrounds and family relationships, vocational aspirations, interests, decisions, school and study, motivation for achievement, etc.). There is also a critique of under-achievement research and studies of underachievers in two different school systems.

Rogers, C. R. My personal growth. In A. Burton and associates, eds., *Twelve Therapists.* San Francisco: Josey-Bass, 1972.

We more than suspect that Dr. Rogers would "cringe" were he to know that his autobiographical paper is listed in a bibliography on underachievement, but we do so, with much admiration and esteem, as an example of incredible growth, self-examination, honesty, and persistence, as factors in Rogers's personal and professional journey. This man's directness and capacity to reveal vulnerabilities is touchingly beautiful. Forgive this word, but you may find this paper inspirational.

Ross, A. O. Learning difficulties in children: dysfunctions, disorders, disabilities. *Journal of School Psychology,* 1967, *5,* 82-92.

Ross's paper is one of a few that is most helpful in discriminating among "different kinds" of difficulties in learning, i.e., the differences between learning disorders, disabilities, and dysfunctions. Learning disorders (similar to a term that Dr. Ross rejects, "primary neurotic learning inhibitions") appear to include the underachiever described by SAI.

Roulet, N. L. Success neurosis in college seniors. *Journal of the American College Health Association,* 1976, *24,* 232-34.

Although Dr. Roulet limits himself to success neurosis (characterized by unconscious fear of surpassing father) in college students, this concept easily applies to younger students as well. Four brief case studies are included. Bricklin and Bricklin (chapter 7) also discuss fear of success.

Sarnoff and Raphael
See above.

Thorndike, R. L. *The Concepts of Over- and Underachievement.* New York: Teachers College Press, 1963.

Challenges the concept of underachievement but, more important in our view, is a magnificent critique of the research methodology in underachievement.

Tape Recording

The Betterlies. Available from the tape library of the American Academy of Psychotherapists. (AAP, 1040 Woodcock Road, Orlando, Florida 32803)

Focuses on one family and their underachieving daughter. We have not heard this particular tape, but the AAP tape library has a deservedly excellent reputation.

Appendix G

What Ever Happened to Underachievement?

Milton Kornrich, Ph.D.

This brief paper is both a question and a comment concerning an issue that has been buzzing unresolved within me. Prior to 1965, when a book I compiled and edited (Kornrich, 1965) was published, this excellent journal* was not in existence nor were a barrage of learning disabilities books. If one examines the required reading list for that relatively "new" graduate or summer institute course, namely, the course in learning disabilities, or if we examine every item in the 186-page *A Two-Thousand Item Bibliography: The Description, Etiology, Diagnosis and Treatment of Children with Learning Disabilities or Brain Damage* (Tymchuk and Knights, 1969), one conclusion is evident: We are either talking about a different group of children, or we are talking about the same children but our theoretical understanding has changed. Or is it merely a change in labeling? (Forgive the word "merely." I realize that for many, labels that are less judgmental are preferable.)

Journal of Learning Disabilities, to which this paper has been sent for possible publication.

Concretely, in 1962-1964, when I reviewed approximately 700 papers on academic underachievement, there was little focus on neurological factors, on minimal brain injury, on perceptual factors, and so on. Now, the shift to this approach is overwhelming, an approach that includes a "certain way" of understanding behavior, which in turn leads to methods of remediation. For example, if the diagnosis is MBD, I cannot think of one specialist who would recommend counseling or psychotherapy as the first priority. This is not a complaint, it's a puzzlement. I am simply uncertain about the meaning and implications of what I am observing.

Now what is my point? Am I merely commenting on current history—a comment anyone in the field could easily make? Am I a disgruntled, psychoanalytically trained and oriented psychologist who is bemoaning the fact that analytic, psychodynamic formulations are now used with lesser frequency to account for problems in learning? Although I am psychoanalytic in training and bias, that cannot be the problem, since I daily use the concept of minimal brain dysfunction. I certainly do believe that perceptual-motor problems can pose a major learning handicap. I do make referrals to pediatric neurologists, perceptual trainers, tutors, and so on. In fact, I have always been interested in what I term the "brain-injured psychologist." The latter is so rigid that anything other than "emotional" or "psychogenic" is either not perceived, or is looked upon with disdain.

So, it is hoped, I am neither making simply an observation about a change in focus, nor am I writing of my pain and distress because "the truth," as I see it, is being avoided. Actually, my concern is that if the shift in understanding and treatment is as dramatic as I believe it to be, many youngsters may get lost in the rush. Surely, if we were heretofore insensitive to, for example, perceptual problems, and indiscriminately recommended psychotherapy and/or tutoring for all learning problems, we were doing a disservice to many children, either out of ignorance or theoretical bias (perhaps another form of ignorance). But now, the reverse may be true. We may now, in our enthusiasm for programs and treatment methods, all of which are certainly needed, "throw in" those children who perhaps, like the under-achiever of old, are primarily passive-aggressive kids showing anger (and dealing with it masochistically—"I'll show you, I'll get me") by lousing up school. After all, if my understanding is correct, psychodynamic concepts are simply concepts; the concept of brain injury is simply a concept, an inference (Birch, 1964).

Confusion Reviewed

The following illustrations, clearly not exhaustive, highlight my confusion, occasionally my enlightenment.

In the recent *Learning Disabilities Guide* (1976), "Children with learning disabilities are defined by the new law as children with a disorder of one or more of the basic psychological processes involved in understanding or using language. Such disorders must be perceptual handicaps, brain injury, minimum brain dysfunction, dyslexia, and developmental aphasia. The definition would not include learning disabilities which stem from emotional disturbance or environmental, cultural, or economic disadvantage."

In McDonald's (Hellmuth, 1968) list (via questionnaire) of twenty-two synonyms for learning disabilities, item no. 22 is "underachievement." Even alphabetically, it's last on the list, but it is on the list. In phase three of the study of minimal brain dysfunction in children (Chalfant and Scheffelin, 1969), in the eight definitions of a learning disability, some definitions include emotional factors (e.g., Kirk), other definitions (e.g., Myklebust) definitely rule out emotional factors ("psychogenecity"), while others (e.g., Bateman) make no mention of it. Farrald and Schamber (1973) also review definitions and conclude, "A child with learning disability is any child who—for whatever reason—consistently fails to meet the demands of the curriculum. . . ."

After reading all the definitions of learning disabilities, in terms of groups included and excluded, I was no longer confused. I was dizzy.

In the case of Harry, reported in this journal (Ables, Aug,

and Leoff, 1971), a dual approach (remedial reading and psychotherapy) was used simultaneously and successfully, with the authors candidly acknowledging their inability to discern whether the child's reading problems were organically or emotionally (or both) based.

Ross's superb paper (1967), in which he skillfully distinguishes between learning disorders, disabilities, and dysfunctions, assisted in de-confusing me to a considerable extent, but note that in the following cogent paragraph we are left with the individual child and his particular needs, as opposed, I would assume, to one approach (e.g., perceptual training, psychopharmacology, psychotherapy, special education, etc.).

> We all too often look for the cause of learning difficulties in the child's personality. Not having found conclusive answers there, our search has carried us in ever-widening circles in the environment. We have studied the child's interaction with his mother, then with his father, later with both parents, and most recently we are looking at family interaction as the source of the difficulty. The next round of this outward search involving the community and society has already begun, but it may be appropriate to question whether we are going in the right direction in this search. Instead of moving ever outward from the child it might be necessary to turn back and look inside the child who is, after all, the learning organism. It may well be that atypical cognitive capabilities are the basis of many of the learning problems which most confound us. The things we are trying to teach and the manner in which we teach them would thus be far more crucial to investigate than some of the child's interpersonal interactions. It is, for example, entirely feasible that a child who has difficulties with his schoolwork has a disrupting influence on the family and not vice versa. Since not all children learn at the same rate or in the same manner, a careful analysis of the individual child's specific learning difficulty should lead to highly individualized remedial efforts.

Anderson (1970), after describing the psychogenic, neurological, and neuropsychogenic models, states, "Our bias leads us to the position that, unless increasing attention is paid to the neglected psychogenic factors, many programs for treating learning disabilities will encounter increasing difficulty with problem learners. Curriculum planning should not ignore the fact that the child is first a social being and his disability cannot exist apart from his evolving self-concept."

Katrina de Hirsch (1963) clearly delineates between a group of adolescents where psychological disturbance is either primary or secondary with respect to learning problems.

Barsch (1968), in a scholarly tour de force, observes that ". . . learning disabilities must not be interpreted as a more palatable and popularly acceptable term for the 'brain-injured child' of ten years ago." Yet, McCarthy and McCarthy (1969) concluded that "the term learning disability began appearing with regularity in the early 1960's largely as a substitute for brain-injured." In a glossary of "Terms Associated with Learning Disabilities" (seventy-four terms), brain damage is listed, as is "emotional blocking"(?). Well, take your choice. 1. Do all learning disorders reflect brain dysfunction? 2. Is underachievement a learning disorder as defined (despite variation in definition)?

In a recent paper by Chalfant and King (1976), "An Approach to Operationalizing the Definition of Learning Disabilities," specificity and clarity are remarkable, but I do not believe that the deficits discussed (e.g., attention, discrimination, memory, sensory integration, concept formation) apply to the group or subgroup of academic underachievers I am referring to. This is further supported by the authors in their paragraph "The Exclusions Factor Component": "The exclusion factor component refers to identifying the handicapping conditions which cause problems in learning other than learning disabilities. These include: mental retardation, visual impairment, hearing impairment, social-emotional problems, physical problems, poor instruction, and cultural or environmental factors." (One might be interested to note that Theodora Abel specifically refers to underachievement among retardates [Abel, 1945].)

If I am correct, the literature above, albeit a "sample," does not help me conclude (1) whether emotional problems, as a primary factor, are subsumed under the term learning disability (the answer appears to be no, but not consistently so); (2) whether underachievement as the term was "originally" used (e.g., Grunebaum et al., 1962; Halpern, 1963; Wallach, 1960) is subsumed under the term learning disability; and (3) if learning disability and brain damage are synonymous, then doesn't type of treatment clearly become an issue? For example, Gardner (1973) for the MBD child recommends, in the following order, medication, education, parental guidance, and psychotherapy. Certainly this sequence of priorities would not be justified for an underachiever without typical MBD symptoms—and that is the "kind" of underachiever I am referring to.

Summary and (In)conclusion

I am genuinely puzzled. I am no stranger to differing schools of thought, whether they apply to achievement, underachievement, or other behaviors, but the literature has so drastically changed in the past ten years that I am left wondering about the underachieving youngster who does not appear to be minimally brain-injured or similarly impaired. He hears, he discriminates, sees, perceives, processes, has no "soft (neurological) signs," and so on. Am I to discount sociological and psychological explanations or their interplay? Or only regard them in most cases as secondary reactions? Perhaps this youngster, "the underachiever of old," is now seen less frequently? One thing is clear, as a diagnostic entity (see APA, DSM, II) and as a source of funding, "underachievement" has less clout. Frankly, I worry less about explanation and the status of a term than I do uniform, anti-eclectic "treatment" for all. Let us not move so vigorously in one direction that we disregard an oft-heard but valid, I feel, clinical cliché—there are several paths to the identical symptom or disorder.

There are still youngsters who are underachieving, in the full spectrum of intellectual capacity, who do not demonstrate— either in their overt behavior or their test responses on psycho-educational evaluation or upon neurological assessment—MBD symptoms. If, as I am informed, MBD has become the most popular child guidance clinic diagnosis, then I believe my concern is proper to attempt to exclude a non-MBD, nonachieving (or Halpern's term, anti-achieving) group.

While some of the papers cited address themselves to the neglect of emotional factors in the LD child, I am beyond and to the side of that issue by questioning whether underachievement properly belongs in the LD classification.

As I write this, I am recalling a seventeen-year-old youngster in an LD class. Psychotherapy had never been considered by his affluent, well-educated parents. They were told he had MBD. Yet, not one multidiscipline evaluation, since age five, by anyone, documents such a diagnosis. The parents feel off the "blame hook," and the kid has been rendered moderately traumatized by his special-class placement. If he is not indeed an MBD child, perhaps the "diagnosis" of underachievement would have prompted other remedial approaches, with at least the youngster's self-esteem more intact.

I hope I have been reasonably clear about both my confusion and concern, and have not confused the reader, especially if my conceptual dilemma was not one the reader initially shared.

REFERENCES

Abel, T. M. The Rorschach test and school success among mental defectives. *Rorschach Research Exchange,* 1945, *9,* 105-10.

Ables, B. S., R. G. Aug, and D. H. Looff. Problems in the diagnosis of dyslexia: a case study. *Journal of Learning Disabilities,* 1971, *4,* 409-17.

Anderson, R. P. A neuropsychogenic perspective on remediation of learning disabilities. *Journal of Learning Disabilities,* 1970, *3,* 143-48.

Barsch, R. H. Perspectives on learning disabilities: the vectors of a new convergence. *Journal of Learning Disabilities,* 1968, *1,* 7-23.

Birch, H. G., ed. *Brain Damage in Children—the Biological and Social Aspects.* Baltimore, Maryland: Williams and Wilkins, 1964.

Chalfant, J. C., and F. S. King. An approach to operationalizing the definition of learning disabilities. *Journal of Learning Disabilities,* 1976, *9,* 228-43.

Chalfant, J. C., and M. A. Scheffelin. *Central Processing Dysfunctions in Children.* Bethesda, Maryland: U.S. Dept. HEW, 1969.

de Hirsch, K. Two categories of learning difficulties in adolescents. *American Journal of Orthopsychiatry,* 1963, *33,* 87-91.

Farrald, R. R., and R. G. Schamber. *A Diagnostic and Prescriptive Technique.* Sioux Falls, South Dakota: ADAPT Press, 1973.

Gardner, R. A. Psychotherapy of the psychogenic problems secondary to minimal brain dysfunction. *International Journal of Child Psychotherapy,* 1973, *2,* 224-56.

Grunebaum, M. G., et al. Fathers of sons with primary neurotic learning inhibitions. *American Journal of Orthopsychiatry,* 1962, *32,* 462-72.

Halpern, H. M. Can psychotherapy help the underachiever? In H. M. Halpern, *A Parent's Guide to Child Psychotherapy.* New York: A. S. Barnes, 1963.

Kornrich, M., ed. *Underachievement.* Springfield, Illinois: Thomas, 1965.

Learning Disabilities Guide. Waterford, Connecticut: Croft-NEI, April, 1976.

McCarthy, J. J., and J. F. McCarthy. *Learning Disabilities.* Boston: Allyn and Bacon, 1969.

McDonald, C. W. Problems concerning the classification and education of children with learning disabilities. In J. Hellmuth, ed., *Learning Disorders,* vol. 3, Seattle, Washington: Special Child Publications, 1968.

Ross, A. O. Learning difficulties in children: dysfunctions, disorders, disabilities. *Journal of School Psychology*, 1967, *5*, 82-92.

Tymchuck, A. J., and R. M. Knights. *A Two Thousand-Item Bibliography: The Description, Etiology, Diagnosis, and Treatment of Children with Learning Disabilities or Brain Damage.* Ottawa, Ontario: Carleton University, 1969.

Wallach, M. A. et al. Relationship of family disturbance to cognitive difficulties in a learning problem child. *Journal of Consulting Psychology*, 1960, *24*, 355-60.